THE SUPREME GUIDE TO WRITING

THE SUPREME GUIDE TO WRITING

JILL BARTON

OXFORD
UNIVERSITY PRESS

OXFORD
UNIVERSITY PRESS

Oxford University Press is a department of the University of Oxford. It furthers
the University's objective of excellence in research, scholarship, and education
by publishing worldwide. Oxford is a registered trade mark of Oxford University
Press in the UK and certain other countries.

Published in the United States of America by Oxford University Press
198 Madison Avenue, New York, NY 10016, United States of America.

Library of Congress Cataloging-in-Publication Data

ISBN 978–0–19–775436–8 (pbk.)
ISBN 978–0–19–775435–1 (hbk.)

DOI: 10.1093/oso/9780197754351.001.0001

Paperback printed by Marquis Book Printing, Canada
Hardback printed by Bridgeport National Bindery, Inc., United States of America

MIX
Paper | Supporting
responsible forestry
FSC
www.fsc.org   FSC® C103567

For Eric

Contents

Acknowledgments

Many colleagues offered advice and support throughout this six-year project. I am especially grateful to my good friend Rachel H. Smith for her unwavering encouragement, and to Christina Frohock, Nancy Levit, Nicole Mariani, Renee Schimkat, Wanda Temm, and my colleagues in the wonderfully supportive legal writing community.

At the University of Miami School of Law, Dean Patricia White, Dean David Yellen, and Vice Dean Drew Dawson were exceptionally supportive. I also owe thanks to these stellar research assistants: James Goodman, Dillon Richards, Alyssa Hoffman, Berta Gonzalez, Evan Robinson, Stephanie Rosner, and Evan Wadler.

My editors at Oxford University Press, David McBride and Sarah Ebel, were helpful throughout the book's production, along with copy editor Joseph Matson and project manager Balaji Padmanaban.

And to the justices of the U.S. Supreme Court, past and present: Thank you for inspiring us all with your words of clarity and compassion.

Introduction: A Supreme Writing Revolution

Great writing anchors great achievements. The founders pledged "life, liberty, and the pursuit of happiness."[1] The first Congress shielded us from "unreasonable searches and seizures" and laws "abridging the freedom of speech, or of the press."[2] Lawmakers since ensured that government would not "deprive any person of life, liberty, or property, without due process of law; nor deny to any person within its jurisdiction the equal protection of the laws."[3] Judges interpret those promises and protect and expand them.

Careless writing, though, can cause misfortune. A hyphen mishap in a tax law once cost the U.S. government $40 million.[4] A realtor who forgot an apostrophe in a social media post faces a defamation lawsuit and a $180,000 legal bill for the trial alone.[5] And a 12-year-old was arrested after using a few emojis that school officials deemed threatening.[6]

Poor writing can cause legal problems even when the writer has nothing to do with the law. Good lawyers can struggle to get it right, often referencing a hodgepodge of books to find answers to grammar and writing style questions. And those answers might be wrong. Maine lawmakers purposefully left out a serial comma in a law about overtime pay because they followed the grammar rule in the state's legislative drafting manual, which references five other guides.[7] But that choice led to confusion and litigation, resulting in a $5 million loss for a dairy farm.[8]

The Supreme Guide to Writing. Jill Barton, Oxford University Press. © Oxford University Press 2024.
DOI: 10.1093/oso/9780197754351.001.0001

What worked for Benjamin Franklin, or just a few decades ago, doesn't work today—he didn't have to grapple with social media and hashtags and the 24-hour news cycle. Writers need a single guide to follow, one that definitively explains the grammar and style rules that matter, and one that describes how to modernize one's writing as language evolves.

This book strives to be that guide, to show you how to be a great writer, even as great writing is a moving target. It takes a deep dive into studying the best: the nine esteemed justices sitting on the U.S. Supreme Court. The justices shape the law, employing language that often sings. They slice through dense wording and speak directly to readers, so anyone can understand what their rulings say. They are unanimously progressive when it comes to language, adjusting and adapting as times change.

In some ways, writing style evolves so swiftly that even the Supreme Court justices disagree on where to change and where to hold true to traditional rules. Some have vaulted toward informality and use contractions, despite Justice Antonin Scalia's complaint they are "intellectually abominable."[9] Some justices write *Congress'* to show the possessive; others write *Congress's*. Some use *because* interchangeably with *since*; some wouldn't dare.

So what rules should you follow?

The Supreme Guide to Writing has the answers, settling grammar and writing style debates the same way the Court does: by pronouncing the majority rule on more than 30 points of legal grammar and style. That means when at least five of nine justices use contractions (as is the case now) that majority rule prevails, finally giving lawyers a clear-cut guideline to follow.

The dissenters have a voice here too. When the justices bend and break grammar and style rules, as good writers do, this book delves into the when, why, and how of their methods. One fault with today's writing style books is they are too rigid. On some points, rigidity is required—as with that costly serial comma. But good writing also calls for flexibility, along with the knowledge of how to contort

one's words around stodgy rules about colons, commas, conjunctions, modifiers, and a host of other grammar and style points. Where
nonconformity is the norm, this guide details the more creative—yet
correct—paths to follow.

The best writing appears effortless, but takes tremendous effort.
Legal writing even more so. There is no room for error, but instead
a demand for nuance, persuasion, transparency, and above all, perfect
clarity. "The world does not expect logic and precision in poetry or
inspirational pop-philosophy;" Scalia wrote, "it demands them in the
law."[10]

Even so, the Court's writing is poetic, inspiring, and instilled with
plenty of pop-culture tidbits and real-life examples that make it ap-
proachable. Writing is an art. You can't just copy a template or a sentence and call it good writing. But you can find inspiration. You can
emulate. You can practice until you find your voice. To help you do
just that, this book has distilled the Court's best writing of late into
hundreds of examples.

This book's rules are amassed from a study of more than 10,000
pages of recent Court opinions that examined how the justices treat
the most essential points of grammar and style, from commas and
conjunctions to pronouns and prepositions. Some rules might shock
or dismay traditionalists. Some will offer helpful reminders on basic
grammar questions, such as how to use an ellipsis or em-dash and
fix common mistakes, like *it's* versus *its* and *who* versus *whom*. Other
guidelines offer a more modern and nuanced approach to follow.

For easy reference, the book is organized into two parts and 32
chapters, one for each grammar or style topic. The first part covers
all punctuation marks, with a how-to on the "intellectually abominable" contraction and a surprising switch on several points, including
the rules for colons and commas. The second part answers questions
about words, from choosing the right conjunction, modifier, pronoun,
or verb, to deciding if you can use a qualifier, double negative, or split
infinitive, or end a sentence with a preposition. (Yes, on all counts.)
Within each section, *The Supreme Guide to Writing* answers questions

looking to the future of language, explaining, for example, what to do with emojis and how to use more inclusive pronouns.

At each step, this guide describes the justices' best tricks: how Justice Elena Kagan achieves simplicity from complexity with plain language; how Justice Neil Gorsuch pulls off an easy swagger; and how Chief Justice John Roberts employs rhythm to bring a story to life. Throughout, the book offers an apolitical look inside the Supreme Court justices' writing style choices, because good writing crosses party lines, and shows exactly how to follow these great writers' leads.

Not all great writers are lawyers, but all great lawyers are great writers. This book is for anyone who strives to be a great writer, or a great lawyer—and those aspiring to be both. Whether you want to keep up with writing trends, polish your style, learn what writing habits to abandon, or just rekindle that spark that made you love writing long ago, this guide aims to light the way.

PART I

Punctuation Marks

I

Apostrophes

The young know the rules, but the old know the exceptions.[1]

—Oliver Wendell Holmes

The apostrophe, a mere tiny swoosh, has confused writing legends including Benjamin Franklin, Thomas Jefferson, William Shakespeare, and Jane Austen, who "massacred" the English language with her use of apostrophes.[2] Invented in 1509 to create an absence or a pause, the much-abused apostrophe stirs so much debate and anguish that grammarians founded the "Apostrophe Protection Society" in 2001.[3] So it's no wonder the Supreme Court justices disagree on how—or even whether—to use apostrophes.

Apostrophes can turn a regular word into a possessive or a contraction, and many legal writers avoid the latter because of its informality. Justice Antonin Scalia was vehemently opposed to contractions. But if you steer clear of these two-word combos nowadays, you're failing to follow the majority rule among current Supreme Court justices. And for possessives, the justices split on whether to write *Congress'* or *Congress's*.

1.1 Contractions: The 8–1 majority rule: Use common contractions within reason.

Using contractions is one of the easiest ways to make writing more conversational. And if you use a contraction on occasion, you'll be in

The Supreme Guide to Writing. Jill Barton, Oxford University Press. © Oxford University Press 2024.
DOI: 10.1093/oso/9780197754351.003.0001

good company. Ten justices since 2018 (eight current justices along with former Justices Stephen Breyer and Ruth Bader Ginsburg) have lightened their writing with contractions. (Even Scalia used a few near the end of his tenure.[4])

But there are limits. Justice Gorsuch sprinkles contractions on nearly every page. But the others use them in strict moderation, mostly in dissents and concurrences, and even then, not in every one they write. A handful of justices (Justices Clarence Thomas, Ginsburg, Breyer, Brett Kavanaugh, and Amy Coney Barrett) have used only one or two in as many years.[5] The takeaway is to use contractions in more personal writings, like emails, letters, and social media posts, and hold off on using them to a large degree in more formal documents that you're writing for clients and courts—who just might hold fast to an old-fashioned, Scalia-era view.

Also, stick with basic contractions: The justices use only common combinations, including *aren't, can't, couldn't, don't, doesn't, isn't, it's, shouldn't, that's, we'll, we're, wouldn't,* and *won't.* They do not use old-fashioned contractions, such as *mustn't, shan't, and 'twas,* along with lesser-known ones: *should've* and *there'd.* And definitely cut out the non-word *ain't.* Chief Justice Roberts even dropped the word when quoting a Bob Dylan lyric in 2008: "When you got nothing, you got nothing to lose."[6]

Roberts later jokingly explained that his version came from the published lyrics because he's "more of a textualist." He added that his version "makes better sense" because otherwise, "it's kind of a double negative."[7]

Contractions can make better sense too. Ginsburg rarely used contractions but did so here to avoid a stilted sentence.

- **Isn't** the Court disarmed from making such a judgment given its recognition that "courts must not presume to determine . . . the plausibility of a religious claim"?[8]

To skirt the contraction, Ginsburg would need to write the clunkier "Is the Court not disarmed . . . ." These next examples from Roberts, along with Justices Breyer, Kagan, and Gorsuch, show how contractions can relieve an otherwise complicated analysis:

- Why **couldn't** Ray's imam receive whatever training in execution protocol the Christian chaplain received? The State has no answer. Why **wouldn't** it be sufficient for the imam to pledge, under penalty of contempt, that he will not interfere with the State's ability to perform the execution? The State **doesn't** say.[9]
- That did not pass muster under this Court's analysis last time. It still **doesn't**.[10]
- If these arguments sound familiar, **it's** because they are.[11]
- With his own experience and their existing relationship in mind, Doe 5 could have reasonably thought that, if this doctor **wouldn't** serve as his covering physician, no one would.[12]
- And surely **that's** a first hint the phrase **wasn't** then a term of art bearing some specialized meaning.[13]
- The unattractive lesson of the majority opinion is this: **What's** mine is mine, and **what's** yours is yours.[14]

Most of the justices use contractions just a handful of times in a year's worth of opinions. Consider that minimalist approach when adding a contraction to your writing. Yes, Gorsuch used one in the first paragraph of his first majority opinion after a long tradition of the Court not doing so.[15] But so far, the justices aren't adopting that avant-garde approach. And while all have signed on to Gorsuch's contraction-filled opinions,[16] Justice Sonia Sotomayor still has not used a single one. The bottom line: if you choose to use a contraction, do so with purpose: to speed the flow of your writing, make a stiff statement conversational, or avoid a clunkier phrase, as Gorsuch (the Court's contraction king) shows here:

- Why **isn't** that enough to demonstrate that today's result **isn't** totally unexpected?[17]

1.2 Possessives.

1.2.1 Unanimous guiding principle: Be consistent: So it's always *Congress's* or always *Congress'* and not a mix of both.

A realtor forgot an apostrophe in a Facebook post, writing *employees* instead of *employee's*. His boss sued for defamation over that forgotten little swoosh, and the trial alone could cost the realtor $180,000 in legal fees.

In the post, the realtor accused his boss of bilking his retirement fund, writing: "Oh Stuart Gan!! Selling multi-million-dollar homes in Pearl Beach but can't pay his *employees* superannuation." As the judge in the case noted, failing to pay one *employee's* retirement "might be seen as unfortunate," but failing "to pay some or all of them looks deliberate."[18]

The rule on possessives has spurred plenty of debate, and not just when apostrophes are missing. For instance, both *Congress'* and *Congress's* are correct, depending on which justice you ask. The justices have long disagreed on how to write the possessive of singular nouns ending in *s*, for words like *Congress*, *process*, and *witness*. Justice Samuel Alito demonstrates this disagreement when, in the same paragraph, he adds an *s* to indicate the possessive for *Congress*, then quotes an older opinion where Justice John Paul Stevens did the opposite:

- In *Raich*, the Court addressed **Congress's** authority to regulate the marijuana market. The Court reaffirmed "**Congress'** power to regulate purely local activities that are part of an economic 'class of activities' that have a substantial effect on interstate commerce."[19]

A 7–2 majority now writes *Congress's*, but that view has flip-flopped. (Justices Anthony Kennedy, Breyer, and Ginsburg wrote *Congress'*. Justices Kavanaugh and Barrett previously have used that shorter version.[20]) All other justices are consistent in their approach, and that rule of consistency is one all writers should follow.

The following examples show the justices' conflicting approach to singular possessives ending in *s*. These first examples show the majority rule.

- Soil near Tammy **Peters's** daycare playground, for example, still shows an arsenic level of 292 ppm.[21]
- In **Kansas's** judgment, that delusion does not make an intentional killer entirely blameless.[22]
- But the court rejected **Lamps Plus's** request for individual arbitration, instead authorizing arbitration on a classwide basis.[23]
- Finally and looking to the law, we know that a **witness's** bare conclusion is regularly held insufficient to meet the substantial evidence threshold—and we know that the government hasn't cited a single case finding substantial evidence on so little.[24]

These next examples skip the extra *s*. While they represent the minority view, they can work when the writer is consistent.

- Under **Kansas'** rule, it can convict the second but not the first.[25]
- Third, **JUSTICE THOMAS'** dissent states that "the Court does not commit" to "which factors are the most important" in determining whether pollutants that enter navigable waters come "from" a point source.[26]
- **Davis'** supervisor at Fort Bend, Kenneth Ford, was well acquainted with Cook.[27]
- This point is the **Achilles'** heel of Barton's structural argument.[28]

1.2.2 Unanimous rule: To make the possessive of a pronoun, skip the apostrophe.

Just to be perfectly clear: *Its* and *your* are possessive pronouns. *It's* and *you're* are contractions. To fix common and annoying apostrophe mix-ups such as these, skip the apostrophe with possessive pronouns. *Hers, his, its, mine, ours, yours,* and *theirs* are all possessive by definition, so they need no apostrophe.

- It is as if my woods are **yours**.[29]
- But, at least in cases like **ours**, it seems the government has chosen instead to continue down the same old path.[30]

Here, Gorsuch demonstrates the distinction between the contractions for *it is* and *you are*, and the similar possessive pronouns.

- This argument suffers from much the same problem as **its** predecessors. . . . And **it's** impossible to *transport* goods without possessing them.[31]
- If you spent **your** career as a state law enforcement officer in West Virginia, **you're** likely to be eligible for a generous tax exemption when you retire.[32]

1.2.3 Unanimous rule: To make the possessive of a singular noun, add an apostrophe plus *s*.

For all other singular nouns, add an apostrophe plus *s*. Under this tried-and-true apostrophe rule, the brief for one petitioner becomes the *petitioner's* brief.

- To be sure, if the monopolistic **retailer's** conduct has not caused the consumer to pay a higher-than-competitive price, then the **plaintiff's** damages will be zero.[33]

1.2.4 Unanimous rule: To make the possessive of a plural noun ending in *s*, add just the apostrophe.

For plural nouns ending in *s*, the standard rule is to add just the apostrophe. Note the difference here from singular nouns ending in *s*, such as the common possessive *Congress's*. For plural nouns that don't end in *s*, like *women* and *men*, add the apostrophe plus *s*.

- And the change in **plaintiffs'** strategy was marked: While state-court litigation of such class actions had been "rare" before the

Reform Act's passage, within a decade state courts were handling most such cases.[34]

- Among these **laws'** provisions were draconian fines for violating broad proscriptions on "vagrancy" and other dubious offenses.[35]
- Ultimately, *Lemon* devolved into a kind of **children's** game.[36]

1.2.5 Unanimous rule: For compound possessives, choose one apostrophe for a joint possessive and two for individual possessives.

These next two rules are for grammarians who like a deep dive. The rule on compound possessives comes up rarely, but it's key to distinguishing how many subjects and objects are involved. Doubling up apostrophes, as in the next example, shows that two or more subjects individually possess their own object.

- And even when two works are substantially similar, if both the **plaintiff's** and the **defendant's** works copy from a third source (reworking, say, a traditional artistic or literary theme), a claim for infringement generally will not succeed.[37]

Two apostrophes—one for the plaintiff and one for the defendant—indicate they have their own individual works. If the plaintiff and defendant co-created their works, the writer would drop the first apostrophe to show they shared the works and ownership: *plaintiff and defendant's works.* To sum up: *Sam and Alex's condominium* indicates a shared home. *Sam's and Alex's condominium* references two units in the same building. The latter option can be awkward, so writing around it is wise.

   When compound subjects are linked with *or* instead of *and*, there's just one apostrophe. That's because *or* makes a compound subject act as a singular one.

- "Until about 1991, when agencies began to change their security policies and practices regarding sexual orientation, there were a number of documented cases where **defense civilian or contractor employees'** security clearances were denied or revoked because of their sexual orientation."[38]

- JUSTICE ALITO imagines a number of ways that Christus may have become aware of **Doe 2 or Doe 3's** abortion practice.[39]

1.2.6 For sticklers, don't italicize the apostrophe-plus-*s* for a possessive case name.

The issue of italicizing the possessive form of a case name came up just a handful of times in as many years. But here's how the justices do it. Note that only the case name is italicized, just as in a citation. The apostrophe and optional *s* are not.

- *Stare decisis*, the doctrine on which **Casey's** controlling opinion was based, does not compel unending adherence to **Roe's** abuse of judicial authority.[40]
- The majority recites **Gingles'** shopworn phrases as if their meaning were self-evident, and as if it were not common knowledge that they have spawned intractable difficulties of definition and application.[41]

But wait: The italics stay if part of the case name, as in *Humphrey's Executor v. United States*:

- He is not an inferior officer, so (the majority says) *Morrison* does not apply; and he is not a multimember board, so (the majority says) neither does **Humphrey's**.[42]

2

Brackets

Start with customary usage.[1]

—Justice Neil Gorsuch

2.1 Unanimous rule: Use brackets in essential quotes to show a change to a word or capitalization.

Brackets let the writer change a quote "abracadabra-style," to borrow a term from Justice Kagan.[2] All the justices use brackets when part of a quote doesn't quite work, making these sharp parenthetical marks a key part of the legal writer's toolkit.

Brackets can add clarity and simplicity because they help writers avoid shoving an ill-fitting quote into their writing. But too many brackets can get clunky, weighing down sentences. The justices strike a balance. Pairs of brackets appear every other page or less, on average. The next examples show that when a quotation is essential, meaning that paraphrasing is not an option, brackets can help.

The technical details: Use brackets to show a change to a word's capitalization or a verb tense or when swapping a term or phrase for something else. Also, brackets—and never ellipses—show a change to the start of a quoted sentence, as these first two rules show.

The Supreme Guide to Writing. Jill Barton, Oxford University Press. © Oxford University Press 2024.
DOI: 10.1093/oso/9780197754351.003.0002

2.2 Unanimous rule: In a quote, use brackets to indicate a change in a word's capitalization to start a sentence.

- After Bartlett was handcuffed, he claims that Nieves said: "**[B]et** you wish you would have talked to me now."[3]
  - *The bracket indicates that the original sentence did not start with "bet."*
- ("**[I]t** is computationally intractable, and thus effectively impossible, to generate a complete enumeration of all potential districting plans. **[Even]** algorithms that attempt to create a manageable sample of that astronomically large universe do not consistently identify an average or median map.")[4]
  - *The brackets show the source began with the lowercase "it." Chief Justice Roberts then adds the word "even" as a transition to begin the next sentence.*

2.3 Unanimous rule: In a quote, when the original text begins a sentence but you move it to the middle of a sentence, use brackets and a lowercase letter to indicate the change.

- Rather, the class had student "prayer leaders" and "**[t]he** prayers that were said in the classroom were said mostly by the students."[5]
  - *"The prayers" begins the original quoted sentence.*

2.4 Unanimous rule: In a quote, use brackets to indicate a change to a verb tense or term.

- And Congress generally "**intend[s]** the full consequences of what it **sa[ys]**"—even if "inconvenient, costly, and inefficient."[6]
  - *The original says "intend" and "said."*

• Whatever might have been thought in *Plessy*'s time, the Brown Court explained, both experience and "modern authority" showed the "detrimental **effect[s]**" of state-sanctioned segregation: It "**affect[ed] [children's]** hearts and minds in a way unlikely ever to be undone."[7]
  ○ *The original says "effect" and "affect their hearts and minds."*
• "The plaintiff must show that the retaliation was a substantial or motivating factor behind the **[arrest]**, and, if that showing is made, the defendant can prevail only by showing that the **[arrest]** would have been initiated without respect to retaliation."[8]
  ○ *The original says "prosecution" instead of "arrest."*

2.5 Unanimous rule: In a quote, use brackets to indicate a change to a phrase.

• Alabama countered that Madison had "a rational understanding of **[the reasons for]** his impending execution," as required by *Ford* and *Panetti*, even assuming he had no memory of committing his crime.[9]
  ○ *The original says "a rational understanding of his impending execution or the reasons for it."*

2.6 The rarely used rule on *sic*: Use brackets and the word *sic* to indicate an error in quoted material.

The term *sic* means "so" or "thus" in Latin and indicates a grammatical error or misspelling in a quote. In five recent years, the justices used *sic* just eight times (hiding three in footnotes) to show they intentionally left the error in a quotation. This rarity shows the justices prefer to paraphrase and correct a mistake, avoiding the need to repeat the error and call out another writer for it. Here, Justice Alito uses *sic* when citing a misspelling from 1701 and Justice Sotomayor uses it to show a grammar error.

- Charter of Privileges Granted by William Penn (1701), in *id.*, at 31–32 (declaring that "no Person ... who shall confess and acknowledge *One* almighty God ... and profess ... themselves obliged to live quietly under the Civil Government, shall be in any Case molested or prejudiced ... because of ... their **consciencious [*sic*]** Persuasion or Practice, nor ... suffer any other Act or Thing, contrary to their religious Persuasion").[10]
- Garza's affidavit states that he wished to argue, at least in part, that he "was persuaded to plead guilty by [the] prosecuting attorney and [his] counsel which was not **voluntarily [*sic*]**."[11]

3

Colons

As I tell people, there are no natural writers. What there are, are writers who have learned their skill and know how to edit.[1]

—Justice Sonia Sotomayor

3.1 Unanimous guiding principle: Use a colon to set off information within a sentence or after an independent clause.

If you get through all 783 pages of Ulysses, it won't be without a lot of breaks. James Joyce helpfully injected many breaks for the reader with colons, and the work has more of these formal punctuation marks than other literary classics.[2] Joyce even crammed 15 colons into a single sentence.[3]

You won't see quite so many from the justices. But you will see them eschew the traditional grammarian rule that colons should follow only independent clauses, as opposed to shorter phrases.[4] All nine justices use colons at a sentence's midpoint to set off a quotation, a rule, a list, or other information. Their only rule is that what follows, whether a phrase or independent clause, is closely related.

The traditional rule can require writers to add the wordy *as follows* or *the following* before a colon.[5] A few justices follow this old practice

The Supreme Guide to Writing. Jill Barton, Oxford University Press. © Oxford University Press 2024.
DOI: 10.1093/oso/9780197754351.003.0003

at times, but all skip that outdated requirement when it better serves their writing.

3.2 Unanimous rule: Use a colon to set off information within a sentence or after an independent clause.

- As the State summarized: "He's not psychotic. He's not delusional."[6]
- The ESA defines "critical habitat" as: "(i) the specific areas within the geographical area occupied by the species . . . on which are found those physical or biological features (I) essential to the conservation of the species and (II) which may require special management considerations or protection; and (ii) specific areas outside the geographical area occupied by the species . . . upon a determination by the Secretary that such areas are essential for the conservation of the species."[7]
- First, however, a caveat: We readily admit that discerning the meaning of "third party bank check" in §2503 is tricky, because the FDA does not define that phrase, and, as far as we can tell, it does not have an "ordinary, contemporary, common meaning."[8]
- So too here: Contrary to the Court's analysis, Congress's use of "any" covers defendants of "whatever kind," including third-party defendants like petitioner.[9]
- No surprise: It encourages us to read the former language as allowing goods to be moved tax-free along local roads to the highways but the latter language as authorizing taxes on the Yakamas' goods once they arrive there.[10]
- But the *Shelton* Court had already explained why the failure to narrowly tailor was problematic: because the statute significantly burdened Arkansas teachers' associational rights.[11]

3.3 Traditional rule: A colon should follow an independent clause.

In that last example, Justice Sotomayor shows that what follows the colon doesn't have to be a complete sentence. What comes before the colon also doesn't have to be an independent clause, despite that old-fashioned rule stating otherwise.[12] But all nine justices still pay homage to the traditional rule of adding a colon after an independent clause, occasionally forcing it by adding an *as follows* or *the following*. This sometimes-adherence to the old ways shows the Court's flexible writing style.

- **To repeat: The Board has broad investigatory powers:** It can administer oaths, issue subpoenas, take evidence and demand data from governments and creditors alike.[13]
- The Court was clear: "We cannot say, as a *constitutional* matter, that in every case counsel's failure to consult with the defendant about an appeal is necessarily unreasonable."[14]
- Putting all these statutory terms together, the rule can be stated **as follows:** A permit is required when a pollutant is "add[ed]" to navigable waters "from" a "point source."[15]
- The plurality's response to this important issue is **the following, portentous sentence:** "The record of the treaty negotiations may not support the contention that the Yakamas expected to use the roads entirely unconstrained by laws related to health or safety."[16]

3.4 Additional rule: Use a colon after a formal salutation.

These double dots aren't just for combining sentences. Colons can also follow formal salutations, with the less formal comma following less formal greetings. Both of the following for a letter or email are correct, depending on how well the writer knows the recipient.

- Dear Judge Rothenberg:
- Dear Leslie,

4

Commas

Be intentional about the words you choose.[1]

—Justice Ketanji Brown Jackson

4.1 Unanimous guiding principle: Use a comma when clarity or cadence compel one.

Back in 1872, a misplaced comma in a tariff law between two simple words—"fruit" and "plants"—cost the government the equivalent of $40 million.[2] Too many other million-dollar comma mistakes have wound their way through the courts since.[3]

If that's not enough pressure for a legal writer, there's also the worry that an imprecise placement of any comma can throw off the flow of your writing, and ruin the forcefulness of your point. As Oscar Wilde noted, "I was working on the proof of one of my poems all the morning, and took out a comma. In the afternoon I put it back again."[4]

The justices seem to keep all this in mind as they drop commas into their drafts. But they also don't follow all the comma rules that other writers might—or that grammarians would insist upon. Let's start with the straightforward: the justices stick with a handful of tried-and-true rules. All use the serial comma. All use commas before a short conjunction combining two independent clauses. All use commas to separate elements in locations and complete dates. And finally, all use commas around parenthetical phrases and nonrestrictive clauses.

The Supreme Guide to Writing. Jill Barton, Oxford University Press. © Oxford University Press 2024.
DOI: 10.1093/oso/9780197754351.003.0004

From here, what to do gets tricky because the justices use commas in what might seem a haphazard fashion. They put commas after introductory words and phrases, but not universally or unanimously. They sometimes add commas around conjunctions in one sentence, but when using the same conjunction in a similar way in the next sentence, they leave it off.

While all this might seem confusing, the bottom line is that the justices use a comma when they need to pause. So consider how you would pace your sentence if you were to speak it aloud. If you pause, add a comma. If not, skip it. The justices take care with the cadence of their writing, and their nonconformity to some traditional comma rules shows this.

As Chief Justice Roberts has said, the cadence of any writing is key: "The pacing—bringing the reader along at the particular speed you want, for the effect you want—is, I think, very important."[5]

These next examples illustrate where the justices place their commas. Each rule in this chapter describes when and how to use a comma. That means if you can't find a rule here to support the comma in a sentence, do the reader a favor and cut it out.

4.2 Unanimous rule: Use a comma before a short conjunction combining two independent clauses.

This rule means that when you take what could be two sentences (a.k.a. independent clauses), and you combine them into one sentence using a short conjunction, you add a comma before the conjunction. The justices universally follow this rule with *and* and *but*. The other coordinating conjunctions—*for, nor, or, so,* and *yet*—work here too, though the justices seldomly use them in this way.

- Warts dot its back**, and** dark spots cover its entire body.[6]
- Nieves approached Bartlett to explain the situation**, but** Bartlett was highly intoxicated and yelled at him to leave.[7]

- That is true of most unconstitutional motive claims**, yet** we generally trust that courts are up to the task of managing them.[8]
- Congress may think these state protections adequate**, or** it may choose to expand the reach of the FDCPA.[9]
- At this early pleadings stage of the litigation, we do not assess the merits of the plaintiffs' antitrust claims against Apple**, nor** do we consider any other defenses Apple might have.[10]
- The passenger's damages for lost wages are not taxable under the RRTA**, for** she has no employment relationship with the railroad.[11]
- Weight claims that Bartlett then stepped very close to him in a combative way**, so** Weight pushed him back.[12]

4.3 Unanimous rule: When a sentence has one subject and two verbs connected with *and*, *but*, or another short conjunction, use a comma only if you want a pause.

On this point, the justices unanimously break from tradition. Grammarians advise to skip the comma when a sentence has one subject and two verbs connected with *and*, but to add a comma if the verbs are connected by *but*.[13] No justice consistently follows that rule. The justices sometimes inject a pause with a comma, and sometimes not. In the next examples, consider the cadence and the relationship between the clauses to understand the justices' decisions to add a comma, or not.

To break down this rule a bit more: note that each sentence has one subject for two verbs. That's different from the examples in the last section, where there are two subjects and two verbs (so essentially two sentences). The previous examples combine two independent clauses, while these combine an independent clause with a dependent one.

- He had sustained no injuries during the episode **and** was released a few hours later.[14]

- He denies being aggressive**, and** claims that he stood close to Weight only in an effort to speak over the loud background music.[15]
- At that point, a judge could try **and** convict him of any violation of the terms of his release under a preponderance of the evidence standard**, and** then sentence him to pretty much anything.[16]
- The parties dispute certain details about the arrest **but** agree on the general course of events, some of which were captured on video by a local news reporter.[17]
- Wall-Street canceled**, but** continued to display articles produced by Fourth Estate.[18]
- We should not purport to advise Congress on how it might exercise its legislative authority**, nor** give our blessing to hypothetical statutes or legislative records not at issue here.[19]
- The catchall "general exceptions clause" neither supersedes **nor** overlays it.[20]
- The dissent commits the same interpretive error as AWF: It focuses on *Campbell*'s paraphrase**, yet** ignores the rest of that decision's careful reasoning.[21]
- Petitioners argue that this and other evidence show that respondents thought that their claims were inaccurate **yet** submitted them anyway.[22]

4.4 The unanimous rule: Use commas after introductory words and clauses when a pause or emphasis is required.

Some writers follow the rule that a comma should follow an introductory clause only when it is four or five or more words.[23] Legal writers also commonly use a comma after a single introductory adverb, such as *however*. Most of the justices consistently use commas after all introductory words and clauses. But on occasion, all current members, plus Justice Breyer, leave off the comma after an introductory word or clause.

This seemingly conflicting approach boils down to the guiding comma principle: add a comma for clarity or cadence, whenever a pause or emphasis is required. The next examples show where the justices skip an introductory comma, add one, or even more.

- **Now** we are asked to imagine that the expert had offered detailed oral testimony about the withheld data.[24]
- **Now,** they are at risk of being held responsible retrospectively for failing to warn about other people's products.[25]
- **Then** a strange thing happened.[26]
- **Then,** in 1939, Sanger initiated the "Negro Project," an effort to promote birth control in poor, Southern black communities.[27]
- **Here** it is clear that the Crow Tribe would have understood the word "unoccupied" to denote an area free of residence or settlement by non-Indians.[28]
- **Here,** West Virginia expressly affords state law enforcement retirees a tax benefit that federal retirees cannot receive.[29]
- **But 12 days before the execution** Mr. Bucklew filed yet another lawsuit, the one now before us.[30]
- **But while hanging could and often did result in significant pain,** its use "was virtually never questioned."[31]
- **But once a year,** upwards of 10,000 people descend on the area for Arctic Man, an event known for both extreme sports and extreme alcohol consumption.[32]
- **But, at Mr. Bucklew's request,** this Court agreed to stay his execution until the Eighth Circuit could hear his appeal.[33]
- **So** Congress again took action.[34]
- **So, we ask,** who is the first taxable licensee?[35]
- **Third, and most centrally,** Congress provided for judicial review of "any final decision of the [agency] made after a hearing."[36]

- **Yet, as the plurality acknowledges,** under its view a tribal member who buys the same coat right over the state line in Portland and then drives back to the reservation will owe no tax—all because of a reserved right to travel on the public highways.[37]
- **So, for example, in the cases described above,** the Government could control only the volume of water necessary for the tribe to farm or the fish to survive.[38]
- The clerk certified that the service packet had been **sent and, a few days later,** certified that a signed receipt had been returned.[39]
- Restricting "compensation" to pay for active service, the Court of Appeals relied on statutory history **and, in particular,** the eventual deletion of two references to pay for time lost contained in early renditions of the RRTA.[40]
- First, a person lacking memory of his crime may yet rationally understand why the State seeks to execute him; **if so,** the Eighth Amendment poses no bar to his execution.[41]

4.5 Unanimous rule: Use the serial comma.

The serial, or Oxford, comma offsets a list of three or more items, whether those items are nouns, verbs, adjectives, adverbs, or phrases. The justices always add a comma to offset items in a list connected by *and* or *or*.

- **Snowmobiles, alcohol, and freezing temperatures** do not always mix well, and officers spend much of the week **responding to snowmobile crashes, breaking up fights, and policing underage drinking.**[42]
- History shows that governments sometimes seek to regulate our lives **finely, acutely, thoroughly, and exhaustively.**[43]

- Congress also classifies crimes as **felonies, misdemeanors, or infractions** based on "the maximum term of imprisonment authorized."[44]

4.6 Unanimous rule: Use commas after the day and year in complete dates.

Using commas to separate the day and year in complete dates is an old standard. In the next sentence, note how only the first date has commas because the second date omits the day:

- The state trial court accepted Mont's guilty pleas on **October 6, 2016,** and set the cases for sentencing in **December 2016.**[45]

4.7 Unanimous rule: Use commas to separate elements in locations.

Another basic one: Use a comma to separate cities from states, countries from continents, or territories, provinces, or states from countries.

- In November 2015, a local police officer in **Mobile, Alabama,** pulled Gamble over for a damaged headlight.[46]
- In the early hours of July 27, 2015, two people burgled the Tongue & Cheek restaurant in **Miami Beach, Florida.**[47]
- About 10 years ago, the IFC financed the construction of a power plant in **Gujarat, India.**[48]

4.8 Unanimous rule: Use commas to separate parenthetical phrases and nonrestrictive clauses.

When the word *which* starts a clause in the middle of a sentence, it gets a comma. Clauses beginning with *which* are nonrestrictive, meaning the words aren't essential to a sentence's meaning, so they are offset by commas. Clauses beginning with *that* are essential—so, no comma.

Roberts says he tries to avoid using *which* and the obligatory comma because "it slows you down . . . It starts to sound like one of those old 19th-century contracts—*which* and *wherefore*. *That* just seems to have a better pace to it. I actually find you can usually get rid of both of them and go with the gerund that, again, is better for pacing."[49] But even Roberts can't avoid using *which* and *that* at every turn. Here, he shows how to place a comma.

- *Gingles* concerned a challenge to North Carolina's multimember districting scheme**, which** allegedly diluted the vote of its black citizens.[50]
- But it does not prohibit laws **that** are discriminatory only in effect.[51]

In the first sentence, the allegation about the scheme is a secondary point, so it's offset by a comma. In the next example, the laws' discriminatory nature is the point, so the two ideas shouldn't be separated with a comma.

This rule can get thorny because *when, where, who, whom,* and *whose* also can introduce clauses that are restrictive or nonrestrictive—so sometimes they get commas, and sometimes not. In essence, the words *when, where, who, whom,* and *whose* can act like either *which* or *that* in a sentence, depending on the sentence's meaning. See Chapter 28 for a how-to on these relative pronouns.

The same decision—to add a comma or not—applies when adding essential versus nonessential identifying information to a sentence. In the first example that follows, identifying the respondent and petitioner is essential to introduce the parties at the start of the opinion. In the next examples, the details between the commas are not essential.

- **Respondent Michael Loos** was injured while working at **petitioner BNSF Railway Company**'s railyard.[52]

- Fourth Estate sued Wall-Street and its owner, **Jerrold Burden,** for copyright infringement.[53]
- Respondent Mony Preap, **the lead plaintiff in the case that bears his name,** is a lawful permanent resident with two drug convictions that qualify him for mandatory detention under §1226(c).[54]
- Bartlett was arrested during "Arctic Man," **a weeklong winter sports festival held in the remote Hoodoo Mountains near Paxson, Alaska**.[55]

One final note on these clauses: While a clause starting with *which* always gets a comma, clauses beginning with *in which*, *by which*, and *for which* do not. The same goes for when *which* begins a sentence.

- In particular, Madison claims that he can no longer recollect committing the crime **for which** he has been sentenced to die.[56]
- After a patent issues, there are several avenues **by which** its validity can be revisited.[57]
- What we have before us is a civil proceeding **in which** Home Depot is not a plaintiff and is being sued.[58]
- **Which** is all well and good, except that under the majority's reasoning, how could it not be?[59]

4.9 Unanimous rule: For a parenthetical phrase, use a comma when you need to pause.

The good news here is you don't need to learn any fussy grammar rules or terms to place your commas correctly. Add a comma where clarity and cadence require one—and only then. In other words, when you need a pause. Writers typically pause around parenthetical words and phrases that explain, interject, modify, or qualify the words around them. Consider the next examples as a guide.

To avoid overusing commas, think about the pacing of your sentence. Roberts has advised, "Some things strike my ear differently, and that's very important. And I'll spend a lot of time trying to get a sentence to read in a way that seems comfortable and well paced and conveys the meaning and isn't choppy."[60] Here are examples of that pro-level pacing.

- Habitat can, **of course,** include areas where the species does not currently live, **given that** the statute defines critical habitat to include unoccupied areas.[61]
- I fear that, **by creating the need for this untested exception,** the unwarranted expansion of the Yakamas' right to travel may undermine rights that the Yakamas and other tribes really did reserve.[62]
- Bartlett's standard would thus "dampen the ardor of all but the most resolute, **or the most irresponsible,** in the unflinching discharge of their duties."[63]
- The parties dispute certain details about the arrest but agree on the general course of events, **some of which were captured on video by a local news reporter.**[64]
- The timber plantations consist of fast-growing loblolly pines planted as close together as possible, **resulting in a closed-canopy forest inhospitable to the frog.**[65]
- For example, the landowners propose a maximum soil contamination level of 15 parts per million of arsenic, **rather than the 250 parts per million level set by EPA.** And the landowners seek to excavate offending soil within residential yards to a depth of two feet **rather than EPA's chosen depth of one.**[66]
- The decision today creates significant uncertainty for the State's continuing authority over any area that touches Indian affairs, **ranging from zoning and taxation to family and environmental law.**[67]

• The House asserts that the financial information sought here—encompassing a decade's worth of transactions by the President and his family—will help guide legislative reform in areas **ranging from money laundering and terrorism to foreign involvement in U.S. elections**.[68]

5

Ellipses

The dissent is able to describe the provision . . . only by resorting to
what might be called imaginative use of ellipsis.[1]

—Justice Antonin Scalia

5.1 Unanimous guiding principle: Use an ellipsis if you remove a quote's middle or end.

In our online world, cutting and pasting is so easy that plenty of
lawyers overload their writing with quotations. The justices don't
do this. When they do insert a quote, they make sure every word
is necessary. Then they make sure to quote every part perfectly,
down to the capitalization and punctuation. If the justices take a
word or phrase out of the middle or end of a quote, an ellipsis fills
the void.

There are a few finicky rules here, depending on whether you de-
lete the beginning, middle, or end of a quote. First, don't put an ellipsis at the beginning of a quote. Use a bracket there instead (see
sections 2.2 and 2.3). Second, use *three* spaced periods to show a
deletion in the middle of a quote. And use *four* spaced periods to
show a deletion at the end. That fourth period? It ends the sentence.
For perfectionists, note that the first period in the series of four
touches the last word only when it indicates the end of the original
sentence.

The Supreme Guide to Writing. Jill Barton, Oxford University Press. © Oxford University Press 2024.
DOI: 10.1093/oso/9780197754351.003.0005

5.2 Unanimous rule: Use three spaced periods to show a deletion to the middle of a quote.

- The "focus" of these courts was "primarily upon . . . matters of strictly local concern."[2]

  ○ The original states: "we have courts the focus of whose work is primarily upon cases arising under the District of Columbia Code and to other matters of strictly local concern."[3]

5.3 Unanimous rule: Use four spaced periods to show a deletion at the end of a quote.

- *Grutter* thus concluded with the following caution: "It has been 25 years since Justice Powell first approved the use of race to further an interest in student body diversity in the context of public higher education. . . . We expect that 25 years from now, the use of racial preferences will no longer be necessary to further the interest approved today."[4]
- "It is absurd a jury should be fined by the Judge for going against their evidence, when he who fineth knows not what it is . . . . [I]f it be demanded, what is the fact?"[5]

5.4 Unanimous rule: Use four spaced periods to show a deletion at the end of a quote, and delete the first space to show the end of a sentence in the original.

If you're paying close attention, you might notice a difference in the last two examples. There's no space after "education" in the first example, but there's a space after "is" in the second. That distinction shows a difference in the originals. The first shows that in a quote of multiple sentences, one sentence ends with "education." The second shows the writer cut off the end of a sentence at "is."

Just to review: In this next one, Chief Justice Roberts deletes the space to show the original sentence ends with "back." (He then deletes a clause beginning the next sentence, shown by the bracket.[6])

- "He also saw Trooper Weight push Bartlett back. . . . [T]he test is whether the information the officer had at the time of making the arrest gave rise to probable cause."[7]

And here, Roberts uses a parenthetical to quote an oral argument, where the speaker continued the sentence.[8]

- ("We're not asking this Court to second-guess or reassess. We say take the North Carolina Supreme Court's decision on face value and as fairly reflecting North Carolina law . . . .").[9]

5.5 Unanimous rule: Use three spaced periods then a comma to show the comma created a clause in a quote.

The need for styling an ellipsis with a comma seldomly comes up— only 50 times in five years. Since this Guide covered commas at length (see Chapter 4), the need for precision here should be clear. So here's the quick lesson on this finicky style point. When the quoted material breaks off a clause with a comma, and the justices quote that portion, they show the ellipsis and then the comma to keep that punctuation break.

- From the mid-1970's to the mid-1980's, "the number of annual fatalities averaged 25,000; by 2014 . . . , the number had fallen to below 10,000."[10]

- Although the second factor, the nature of Goldsmith's copyrighted work (creative and unpublished), "would ordinarily weigh in [her] favor . . . , this factor [was] of limited importance because the Prince Series works are transformative."[11]
- Consider the "purposes" listed in the preamble paragraph of §107: "criticism, comment, news reporting, teaching . . . , scholarship, or research."[12]

6

Em–dash

The "best system" full stop—no ifs, ands, or buts of any kind relevant here.[1]

—Justice Elena Kagan

6.1 Unanimous rule: Use an em–dash to emphasize information in the beginning, middle, or end of a sentence.

Grammarians scold the em–dash as an "embarrassing best friend," a crutch for scatterbrained writers, and a sign of "a profusion of overstuffed and loosely constructed sentences, bulging with parenthetical additions and asides."[2] Given this distaste, a cautious writer might be wise to avoid them.

But the justices are more adventurous. They drop hundreds of these powerful punctuation marks in their opinions each term. This long dash offers a punchy alternative to the formal colon, the deemphasizing parentheses, and the more casual comma.

Use two em–dashes to surround information in the middle of a sentence, or one to underscore details at the beginning or end of a sentence. Style here matters: the justices and lawyers everywhere avoid adding spaces before or after an em–dash, unlike what you'll see in journalism or publishing. The justices demonstrate:

• The Court then—quite sensibly—remanded the case to the South Carolina Supreme Court to resolve that question.[3]

The Supreme Guide to Writing. Jill Barton, Oxford University Press. © Oxford University Press 2024.
DOI: 10.1093/oso/9780197754351.003.0006

- The familiar symbol of the Red Cross—a red cross on a white background—shows how the meaning of a symbol that was originally religious can be transformed.[4]
- That provision—call it the Intellectual Property Clause—enables Congress to grant both copyrights and patents.[5]
- The amphibian *Rana sevosa* is popularly known as the "dusky gopher frog"—"dusky" because of its dark coloring and "gopher" because it lives underground.[6]
- No, it exposed all States to the hilt—on a record that failed to show they had caused any discernible constitutional harm (or, indeed, much harm at all).[7]

7

Emoticons and Emojis

A person gets from a symbol the meaning he puts into it, and what is
one man's comfort and inspiration is another's jest and scorn.[1]

—Justice Robert H. Jackson

7.1 Unanimous rule: Avoid emojis and emoticons (but they might find a place in a quote).

"A good opinion has personality," Justice Scalia once said,[2] and he
injected plenty of personality in his dissents with eye-rolling sarcasm.
Scalia stopped short, of course, of dropping a literal eye-roll with an
emoji or emoticon, and every legal writing expert would tell you to
do the same.

But some lawyers and judges must contend with emoticons and
emojis. In one case, two defendants are appealing their convictions re-
lating to the January 6, 2021, insurrection at the United States Capitol,
in part, because the emojis in their text messages weren't admitted into
evidence. The defendants argued, "the Court would have found three
of their communications to reflect sarcasm if the emojis included in
them had been admitted."[3] (This argument did not carry the day. The
Court denied their motions for acquittal and a new trial.[4])

There are dozens more examples. Another federal appeals court
upheld a defendant's conviction for enticing a minor to engage in
criminal activity, partially because of the "romantic emoticons" he
sent.[5] A Massachusetts court affirmed a defendant's conviction of pre-
meditated homicide, over accidental death, because he messaged an

The Supreme Guide to Writing. Jill Barton, Oxford University Press. © Oxford University Press 2024.
DOI: 10.1093/oso/9780197754351.003.0007

emoji with X's for eyes and the victim's nickname.[6] And in Virginia, a 12-year-old was charged with threatening her school after posting a message with a gun, bomb, and knife emoji.[7]

Guidance on how to use emojis and emoticons is lacking in legal writing guides, perhaps because the terms didn't exist when some style guides were written[8] or perhaps they're trying to will the subject away. But emoticons and emojis persist in legal writing, especially in emails, texts, and other online communications.

For the less tech-savvy, here's some background: The word *emoticon* is already outdated. An emoticon is the text-based representation of an emoji. It's what you make when you combine, say, a colon with a closed parentheses to create a smile. Emojis are the smiley face graphic and similar images.

The justices do not use emoticons or emojis (#obviously), though one reference to an emoji appeared in a 2021 free speech case about student profanity on social media.[9] But with the lower courts already grappling with the graphics' meanings and admissibility, the Court is likely to see more of these enigmatic graphics in the future.

Emojis are, admittedly, hard to interpret. In reviewing whether emojis in a blog post were harassment, the Colorado Supreme Court described the difficulty: "Complicating things further, emojis may look different depending on the sender's or recipient's operating system. For one example, an emoji that resembles a toy squirt gun in a message sent on one platform may appear as a revolver on a recipient device."[10]

The unanimous rule here is to use words, not combinations of punctuation marks and numbers, to make your point. If you must refer to an emoji or emoticon because it is part of a legally salient fact, then use both the symbol and real words to describe what it means. The Michigan Court of Appeals demonstrates:

• [A] ":P" emoticon is used to represent a face with its tongue sticking out to denote a joke or sarcasm.[11]

8

En-dash

This is plain to see, for all who do not look the other way.[1]

—Justice Sonia Sotomayor

8.1 Unanimous rule: Use the en-dash to show a range.

This mid-sized dash is left over from typesetting days, when it made reading a range of numbers easier. But today, few writers take the time (or even know how) to create this dash that's technically the size of an *N*—as opposed to the emphasizing em-dash, which is the size of a capital *M*. Or as opposed to the hyphen—the simple, small dash used to combine words. (See Chapter 10 for more on that.) Even so, when the *Chicago Manual of Style* considered getting rid of the en-dash for a recent edition, internet discussion groups erupted in protest, enough to make the *Manual*'s editors retreat.[2]

The justices are old-fashioned here and use all three dashes in their published opinions. The en-dash is used to indicate a range, typically of dates or numbers, and is most common in citations. Here's an illustration of the three types of dashes in a date range. The style on the first and last examples is technically incorrect.

- 2019-2020 Hyphen: Use with compound words and prefixes. See Chapter 10. [Too short]
- 2019–2020 En-dash: Use between numbers, as seen here. [Correct style]

The Supreme Guide to Writing. Jill Barton, Oxford University Press. © Oxford University Press 2024.
DOI: 10.1093/oso/9780197754351.003.0008

- 2019—2020 Em-dash: Use between phrases for emphasis. See Chapter 6. [Too long]

If you want to get out a ruler and measure millimeters of difference, you'll see only the middle example is the correct length, technically speaking. While the Court is precise on the length of these marks, in practice, most lawyers use just two dashes: a hyphen between words and numbers and the longer em-dash for emphasis between words or phrases. Even so, here's where the justices employed the en-dash in recent terms—in dates, page ranges, and proper nouns that include numbers.

- But across the five elections at issue in this litigation (**2008–2016**), Arizona threw away far more out-of-precinct votes—almost 40,000—than did any other State in the country.[3]
- See T. Anbinder, Nativism and Slavery: The Northern Know Nothings and the Politics of the 1850s, pp. **6–8** (1992).[4]
- Shannon is a small town of about 2,000 in northern Mississippi near Tupelo, about halfway between Memphis and Birmingham off **I–22**.[5]
- Using a federal work-authorization form (**I–9**), employers "must attest" that they have "verified" that an employee "is not an unauthorized alien" by examining approved documents such as a United States passport or alien registration card.[6]

9

Exclamation Marks

Legalese—you mean jargon? Legal jargon? Terrible! Terrible! I would
try to avoid it as much as possible. No point. Adds nothing.[1]

—Justice Stephen Breyer

9.1 Guiding principle: Avoid exclamations; but when quoting an exclamation is necessary, put the mark inside the quotation marks.

One character on every keyboard has the power to shout, gesticu-
late wildly, and bark.[2] But this character—the exclamation mark—is
practically forbidden in the civilized world of the law. Exclamation
marks in Supreme Court opinions are so rare it's as if the justices are
following writer Elmore Leonard's advice: "You are allowed no more
than two or three per 100,000 words of prose."[3]

9.2 The 5–4 majority rule: Avoid exclamations.

While the justices nearly unanimously avoid the uncivilized exclamation, some fulfill a rare need to raise the volume. Four justices have
used an exclamation mark to express extreme sarcasm or frustration in
five recent years—but just ten times in over 10,000 pages. So it's wise
to follow the Court's lead and (nearly always) skip this loud punctuation mark.

The Supreme Guide to Writing. Jill Barton, Oxford University Press. © Oxford University Press 2024.
DOI: 10.1093/oso/9780197754351.003.0009

If you must, here's how they've done it. In the first example, Justice Alito also makes up a word—"chango"—to call out the majority's nonsense. In the second, he uses a triple exclamation mark, adding quotes to emphasize the sarcasm. The last one is from a joint dissent by Justices Breyer, Sotomayor, and Kagan.

- If §§922(g) and 924(a)(2) are arbitrarily combined in the way that petitioner prefers, then, presto chango, they support petitioner's interpretation. **What a magic trick!**[4]
- Perhaps the Court thinks the CCA should have used CAPITAL LETTERS or bold type. Or maybe it should have added: **"And we really mean it!!!"**[5]
- In a single sentence, the majority huffs that "nobody disputes" various of these "points of law." **Excellent!** I only wish the majority would take them to heart, both individually and in combination.[6]
- Of course, the majority opinion refers as well to some later and earlier history. On the one side of 1868, it goes back as far as the 13th **(the 13th!)** century.[7]

9.3 Unanimous rule: When quoting an exclamation, the mark goes inside the quote.

Most exclamations in Supreme Court opinions are in quotations and titles. Even these are rare—just a dozen in five years. The style rule here is straightforward: When quoting an exclamation, take care to put the mark inside the quotation. To do the opposite would indicate the writer added the exclamation to yell, which of course, legal writers should not do.[8]

- One especially eager participant played a modern-day Paul Revere, riding on horseback through the crowd to deliver the message: **"The Feds are coming! The Feds are coming!"**[9]

- As has been the case before in the history of American democracy, "the arc of the moral universe" will bend toward racial justice despite the Court's efforts today to impede its progress. Martin Luther King **"Our God is Marching On!"** Speech (Mar. 25, 1965).[10]

10

Hyphens

The hyphen makes that clear.[1]

—Justice Antonin Scalia

10.1 Unanimous guiding principle: Hyphenate compound adjectives, prefixes, and other words for clarity.

When Justice Scalia was an editor on the *Harvard Law Review*, he learned how to use hyphens with the example of the "purple people eater." He explained: "If it's a purple eater of people, you would write it 'purple people, hyphen, eater,' right? And you would understand that: a purple people-eater. On the other hand, if it was an eater of purple people, the hyphen would be moved over: 'purple-people eater.'"[2]

  Scalia said the example "helps comprehension, and anything that helps comprehension should be embraced."[3] The justices embrace hyphens for the same reason, adding one when it aids comprehension, and skipping it when it does not, sometimes, even artfully:

- And, again as with the ACCA, we held that §16's residual clause was unconstitutionally vague because it required courts "to picture the kind of conduct that the crime involves in the ordinary case, and to judge whether that abstraction presents some **not-well-specified-yet-sufficiently-large** degree of risk."[4]

Justice Kagan penned this six-word compound adjective in 2018, and Justice Gorsuch quoted it a year later. The phrase shows how an

The Supreme Guide to Writing. Jill Barton, Oxford University Press. © Oxford University Press 2024.
DOI: 10.1093/oso/9780197754351.003.0010

effective hyphen adds clarity to a series of words that might otherwise be misread. It also shows the justices follow grammatical tradition when using a hyphen, using one with a compound adjective only when it (1) can't be combined into one word, (2) comes before the noun it modifies, and (3) could be misread without a hyphen.

10.2 Unanimous rule: Hyphenate prefixes and compound adjectives that can't be combined into one word.

Stylistically, the hyphen is a short dash (shorter than both the em-dash and en-dash; see Chapters 6 and 8). While an em-dash separates phrases, and the en-dash separates numbers, the hyphen separates words or a word and a prefix. Examples include *anti-discrimination*, *co-fiduciaries*, *cross-examination*, *non-unanimous*, and *pre-existing*. Justice Thomas uses both types of hyphenated words (and a couple em-dashes) here:

- I do not deny that a judge **pre-disposed** to distrust the Secretary or the administration could arrange those facts on a corkboard and—with a jar of pins and a spool of string—create an **eye-catching** conspiracy web.[5]

A hyphen always belongs with a prefix, as with "an un-*Mirandized* confession."[6] But it doesn't always belong in word combinations. Here, Justice Kavanaugh doesn't want you to read about the government's debt, but about the exception for it:

- The Court of Appeals therefore invalidated the **government-debt exception** and severed it from the robocall restriction.[7]

Some compound adjectives have become single words and need no hyphen. Examples of these "closed compounds" that let you save a space include *classwide*, *decisionmaker*, and *healthcare*. When in doubt, look it up. Compound words are uniformly recognized in dictionaries.

Mother-in-law, for example, won't appear in a dictionary without the hyphens, but *precondition* and *commonplace* have none.[8]

10.3 Unanimous rule: Hyphenate compound modifiers only when they precede what they modify.

In "eye-catching conspiracy web," the hyphenated compound modifier comes before the noun phrase it modifies. If Thomas had written, "the conspiracy web was eye catching," thus putting the modifying phrase after "conspiracy web," there would be no hyphen. The meaning is clear in either version, but only the original gets the hyphen because the compound modifier precedes the noun. Here are a few more examples where the justices use complex and doubled-up compound modifiers—always before the noun or phrase they modify:

- Sometimes, he would point the **short-barreled shotgun** in her face.[9]
- In other words, under the Court's unprecedented **three-step framework**, no statute can reach relevant conduct abroad, no matter the true object of the statute's solicitude.[10]
- In this case, we consider the constitutionality of a Louisiana statute, Act 620, that is almost **word-for-word identical** to Texas' **admitting-privileges law**.[11]
- The Constitution's meaning is fixed, not some **good-for-this-day-only** coupon, and a practice consistent with our nation's traditions is just as permissible whether undertaken today or 94 years ago.[12]
- In enacting the original Voting Rights Act in 1965, Congress copied this definition almost verbatim from Title VI of the Civil Rights Act of 1960—a law designed to protect access to the ballot in jurisdictions with patterns or practices of denying such access based on race, and which cannot be construed to authorize **so-called vote-dilution** claims.[13]

10.4 Unanimous rule: Hyphenate words for clarity—when they could be misread without the hyphen.

This hyphen rule is tricky because it requires recognizing when a hyphen is necessary—and not—for clarity's sake. So here's a quick rundown: Cut the hyphen with proper nouns, foreign terms, and word combinations commonly understood as a modifying phrase, a.k.a. open compounds. Open compounds, like *due process* and *prima facie*, do not get a hyphen because when a lawyer writes *due process analysis* or *prima facie case*, the meaning is clear without the hyphen weighing down the sentence.

In the next example, Gorsuch hyphenates *separation-of-powers* but not *due process*, even though both are modifying the noun *principles*. In the second sentence, Justice Alito shows how to skip the hyphen with proper nouns.

- Employing the avoidance canon to expand a criminal statute's scope would risk offending the very same **due process** and **separation-of-powers principles** on which the vagueness doctrine itself rests.[14]
- These include a **World War II** Honor Scroll; a **Pearl Harbor** memorial; a **Korea-Vietnam** veterans memorial; a **September 11** garden; a **War of 1812** memorial; and two recently added **38-foot-tall** markers depicting British and American soldiers in the Battle of Bladensburg.[15]

In short, add a hyphen when you want a phrase read together, as Chief Justice Roberts shows here:

- Instead, they have been hashed out in the "**hurly-burly**, the **give-and-take** of the political process between the legislative and the executive."[16]

10.5 Majority rule: Hyphens typically don't follow words ending in *-ly*.

Purists advise to skip the hyphen with a word ending in *-ly*, and most justices heed this rule (save for the occasional quotation).[17] That's because the modifying purpose of a word ending in *-ly* is typically clear. (This understanding doesn't apply to non-modifying words also ending in *-ly* such as *daily, early, family*, etc.)

Even so, a few justices have put a hyphen after an *-ly* word for clarity on occasion, particularly with a more complicated phrase, such as "not-well-specified-yet-sufficiently-large degree of risk." This departure from the traditional rule shows that clarity sometimes demands a writer break the rules. Here, Justices Alito, Kagan, and Ketanji Brown Jackson do just that:

- The Departments responded by issuing a new regulation that attempted to codify our holding by allowing **closely-held** corporations to utilize the accommodation.[18]
- Yet in each of those elections, Democrats have won (you guessed it) 7 of 8 House seats—including the **once-reliably-Republican** Sixth District.[19]
- This is so because the entire point of *Garmon's* **arguably-protected** test is to permit the court to assess the facts and relevant labor law in service of a *gatekeeping* function.[20]

10.6 Majority rule: For split compound modifiers, add a floating hyphen, if you must.

This finicky grammatical construction with a floating hyphen is so awkward that most justices avoid it most of the time. But getting the style right can mean getting your point right. When using the same adjective to modify multiple words in a series, the second (and third and fourth) word gets a floating hyphen prefix. This hyphen indicates that the modifier applies to the latter words too.

- But here, the panel majority held that this additional freedom did "not apply to off-campus speech," which it defined as "speech that is outside **school-owned, -operated, or -supervised** channels and that is not reasonably interpreted as bearing the school's imprimatur."[21]
- Recall that the exception at issue here concerns debt collection— specifically a method for collecting **government-owned or - backed debt.**[22]

In the first example, the bolded phrase should be read *as school-owned, school-operated, or school-supervised*. In the second, the hyphen floating before *backed* connects it to the modifier *government*. One could just as easily—and correctly—write *government-owned or government-backed debt*. It's a touch wordier, but a touch less technical. That's the choice the justices make most of the time, so you should, too.

11

Parentheses

The parentheses cannot bear that much weight, given the compelling textual evidence to the contrary.[1]

—Justice Antonin Scalia

11.1 Unanimous rule: Use parentheses around a word, phrase, or clause to add an aside.

Justice Ginsburg credited her European literature professor, Vladimir Nabokov, for changing "the way I read and the way I write. Words could paint pictures, I learned from him. Choosing the right word, and the right word order, he illustrated, could make an enormous difference in conveying an image or an idea."[2] Ginsburg took cues from her professor on how punctuation influences the cadence of writing, like how Nabokov used parentheses to slip in some digressions in the opening of *Lolita*:

> My very photogenic mother died in a freak accident **(picnic, lightning)** when I was three, and, save for a pocket of warmth in the darkest past, nothing of her subsists within the hollows and dells of memory, over which, if you can still stand my style **(I am writing under observation)**, the sun of my infancy had set: surely, you all know those redolent remnants of day suspended, with the midges, about some hedge in bloom or suddenly entered and traversed by the rambler, at the bottom of a hill, in the summer dusk; a furry warmth, golden midges.[3]

Commas call on the reader to take note, em-dashes shout, but parentheses whisper. Like Nabokov, all the justices occasionally use

The Supreme Guide to Writing. Jill Barton, Oxford University Press. © Oxford University Press 2024.
DOI: 10.1093/oso/9780197754351.003.0011

parentheses to inject some detail as an aside. They also, like all lawyers, regularly include parentheticals within citations.

Parentheses can surround a word, phrase, or clause at the middle or end of the sentence. Here Justices Kagan and Gorsuch have some fun and show the proper style.

- The first part of that definition, identifying the kind of things covered, is broad: It encompasses words **(think "Google")**, graphic designs **(Nike's swoosh)**, and so-called trade dress, the overall appearance of a product and its packaging **(a Hershey's Kiss, in its silver wrapper)**.[4]
- And we must construe the elements clause as it is—without first inserting the word that will **(presto!)** produce the dissent's reading.[5]
- If asked by a friend **(rather than a judge)** why they were fired, even today's plaintiffs would likely respond that it was because they were gay or transgender, not because of sex.[6]
- The next clause **(but don't get attached: it will soon be superseded)** set out the procedures the electors were to follow in casting their votes.[7]
- That meant the leaders of the era's two warring political parties— the Federalists and the Republicans—became President and Vice President respectively. **(One might think of this as fodder for a new season of Veep.)**[8]

With parentheticals, period placement matters. Note the different placement in these four examples:

- Then try writing out instructions for who should check the box without using the words man, woman, or sex **(or some synonym)**.[9]
  - *A single period outside the parentheses shows the parenthetical is an incomplete clause contained within the sentence.*

- They and their wives sued the equipment manufacturers in Pennsylvania state court. **(McAfee and DeVries later died during the course of the ongoing litigation.)**[10]
  - *Periods end each sentence. The second period goes inside the parentheses to show the parenthetical sentence is contained within.*
- This concern is scarcely hypothetical. *See* Brief for American Civil Liberties Union et al. as *Amici Curiae* 7 **("Perhaps because they are politically easier to impose than generally applicable taxes, state and local governments nationwide increasingly depend heavily on fines and fees as a source of general revenue.").**[11]
  - *Three periods: The first after "hypothetical" ends the first sentence. The second period goes inside the parentheses to show a complete parenthetical sentence is contained within. The third period ends the citation sentence.*
- According to the ALJ, Biestek was entitled to benefits beginning in May 2013, when his advancing age **(he turned fifty that month)** adversely affected his ability to find employment.[12]
  - *There's no period for this complete parenthetical clause because it's an aside within the larger sentence.*

12

Periods

I would gladly stop there.[1]

—Justice Clarence Thomas

12.1 Unanimous rule: Periods end any point, whether it's a complete sentence or not.

"True enough."[2] "Tough as a three-dollar steak."[3] "Pure applesauce."[4] The justices revel in the chance to pack a punch, especially when they quip a pithy phrase that is not quite a sentence. All the justices add fragments, on occasion, to make a point. As Justice Gorsuch might say, when a writer breaks the rule requiring sentences to have a subject and verb, that's "where the magic happens."[5]

In writing, the comma creates a brief pause; the semicolon, a touch longer; the colon, a tough longer than that. Then there's the all-powerful period, the full stop. Periods have a few extra jobs in legal writing. This essential punctuation mark ends fragments and sentences, of course, but it also ends citations and point headings in motions and briefs. Groups of periods—three and sometimes four—create ellipses. (See Chapter 5 for more on ellipses and Chapter 14 for a reminder to always put the period inside quotation marks.)

"Not so" is a favorite fragment among the justices—and exemplifies the pithiness often conveyed in a sentence cut short by design. It has appeared two dozen times in five recent years, in opinions by Chief Justice Roberts and Justices Thomas, Breyer, Sotomayor, Kagan, and Gorsuch.

The Supreme Guide to Writing. Jill Barton, Oxford University Press. © Oxford University Press 2024. DOI: 10.1093/oso/9780197754351.003.0012

- Blackbeard and most of his crew escaped without harm. **Not so the *Revenge*.**[6]
- Last, the Court objects on policy grounds that hewing to the statutes' plain meaning would have "striking implications for federalism and private property rights." **Not so.**[7]

Here are a few more fragments showing that Supreme Court verve.

- This case is about dog toys and whiskey, two items seldom appearing in the same sentence. Respondent VIP Products makes a squeaky, chewable dog toy designed to look like a bottle of Jack Daniel's whiskey. **Though not entirely.**[8]
- The majority does not disagree that the safe-berth clause confers these duties and rights. **Quite the opposite.**[9]
- For the first time ever, this Court refuses to remedy a constitutional violation because it thinks the task beyond judicial capabilities. **And not just any constitutional violation.**[10]
- You know that he reframed and reformulated—in a word, transformed—images created first by others. **Campbell's soup cans and Brillo boxes. Photos of celebrity icons: Marilyn, Elvis, Jackie, Liz—and, as most relevant here, Prince.**[11]
- Carrying out that rule because an employee is a woman *and* a fan of the Yankees is a firing "because of sex" if the employer would have tolerated the same allegiance in a male employee. **Likewise here.**[12]
- **Exactly right and exactly on point in this case.**[13]

13

Question Marks

It's great to be in the position of asking questions and not having to
answer questions.[1]

—Justice Ruth Bader Ginsburg

13.1 Unanimous rule: Question marks state
the issue and belong inside quotation marks
only if part of the original.

"What goods belong in our stores?"[2] What are the limits to voting
restrictions? Should college athletes be paid? Is off-campus student
speech protected? Can juvenile offenders be sentenced to die in
prison? These are just a few of the landmark questions the Court an-
swered in recent terms. Questions keep the legal world humming. As
Chief Justice Charles Evans Hughes noted,

> "How amazing it is that, in the midst of controversies on every con-
> ceivable subject, one should expect unanimity of opinion upon dif-
> ficult legal questions! In the highest ranges of thought, in theology,
> philosophy and science, we find differences of view on the part of the
> most distinguished experts,—theologians, philosophers and scientists.
> The history of scholarship is a record of disagreements. And when we
> deal with questions relating to principles of law and their applications,
> we do not suddenly rise into a stratosphere of icy certainty."[3]

The Supreme Guide to Writing. Jill Barton, Oxford University Press. © Oxford University Press 2024.
DOI: 10.1093/oso/9780197754351.003.0013

13.2 Unanimous rule: Question marks state issues and hypotheticals.

The question mark defines the gray, the undetermined. Typically, judges pose questions and lawyers answer them. So while question marks are a natural part of the justices' opinions, they're scarcer in lawyers' motions and briefs. In five recent terms, the justices employed about 1,800 question marks, stating the issues as questions, posing a rhetorical query or hypothetical, or disputing their colleagues' analyses. Justice Gorsuch, who poses more questions than any other justice (552 in five years compared to Chief Justice Roberts' 48), demonstrates here with a dozen hypotheticals:

- **Not yet convinced?** Consider some tweaks to the Court's hypothetical. Suppose that, instead of misrepresenting the cut of its steaks, a restaurant charged a customer for an appetizer he ordered that never arrived. **What about an appetizer he never ordered? An additional entrée? Three? Three plus a $5,000 bottle of Moët? How about a Boeing 737?** Now suppose the restaurant ran the customer's credit card for the same steak twice. **What if it waited an hour to do so? A day? A year? What if the waiter gave the credit card information to a different employee at the same restaurant to run the charge? A different employee at a different restaurant? What if the restaurant sold the customer's credit card information on the dark web, and another restaurant ran the card for filet mignon?** On the Court's telling, the "crux" of the fraud in some of these examples lies merely in "how and when services were provided," while in others the "crux" involves "who received the services." **But how to tell which is which?**[4]

13.3 Unanimous rule: Question marks belong inside quotation marks only if part of the original.

Using question marks becomes tricky only when a quotation is involved. If a question mark is part of the quoted text, it belongs inside the quotation marks. Justice Breyer shows that placement here where he quotes a question:

- "Finland," for example, is often not the right kind of answer to the question, "Where have you come **from?**" even if long ago you were born there.[5]

But in the next example, Breyer poses a question that ends by quoting a term from a dictionary, so the question mark goes outside the quotation.[6]

- But what does it mean to be like a **"brute animal"**?[7]

14

Quotation Marks

> The plurality tries to suggest a reason by sprinkling its opinion with
> quotations from venerable sources, but all are far afield.[1]
>
> —Justice Samuel Alito

14.1 Unanimous rule: When essential, quote, and keep quotes exact.

When asked their favorite writer, most of the current justices name
the same one: Justice Robert H. Jackson, who served from 1941 to
1954 and was renowned for a candid and seemingly effortless style.[2]
Jackson showed that simple, straightforward way of writing in his le-
gendary *Korematsu v. United States* dissent, arguing against the government's decision to move Japanese Americans into relocation camps
after the bombing at Pearl Harbor.

In that dissent, Jackson wisely used his own words over the words
of others, including just three quotations. First, he quoted the constitutional provision on treason, then a phrase from Judge Benjamin
N. Cardozo about overstepping or "the tendency of a principle to
expand itself to the limit of its logic." Third, Jackson quoted from
Hirabayashi v. United States, the precedent the majority used to jus-
tify its now-unconstitutional decision. All of Jackson's quotations in
Korematsu are essential. And all led Jackson to prove the point that
the majority was extending *Hirabayashi* to "decide the very things we
there said we were not deciding."

He continued:

The Supreme Guide to Writing. Jill Barton, Oxford University Press. © Oxford University Press 2024.
DOI: 10.1093/oso/9780197754351.003.0014

"Because we said that these citizens could be made to stay in their homes during the hours of dark, it is said we must require them to leave home entirely; and if that, we are told they may also be taken into custody for deportation; and if that, it is argued they may also be held for some undetermined time in detention camps. How far the principle of this case would be extended before plausible reasons would play out, I do not know."[3]

It took 74 years for the Court to validate Jackson's argument, when Chief Justice Roberts declared the *Korematsu* order "morally repugnant."[4] The lesson here, beyond the legal ruling, is that when it comes to quotes, fewer is better. As Jackson showed, quote only what's essential.

The unanimous rule here is to use quotation marks only when necessary. That includes just three kinds of quotes:

(1) Constitutional and statutory provisions at issue;
(2) Key parts of caselaw; and
(3) The occasional, artful, on-point phrase (note all the qualifiers here).

The justices avoid dumping quotations or adding anything beyond what's essential, using four or five quotations per page, on average. Beyond that, the rules for quotations revolve around placing those little swooshes and your other punctuation marks correctly.

14.2 Unanimous rule: Use quotation marks when quoting key words and phrases.

Key legal terms and short phrases merit quotation marks. Here, the current Justice Jackson (Ketanji Brown Jackson) uses quotation marks to show which words are at issue.

- Characterizing this **"windfall"** as unfair, Pennsylvania filed an action that asked us to reconsider Texas's escheatment rules.[5]
- The parties have identified four MoneyGram products as relevant to this litigation. MoneyGram calls these financial instruments

**"Retail Money Orders," "Agent Check Money Orders,"
"Agent Checks," and "Teller's Checks."**[6]

- The majority starts its interpretation of the encouragement
  provision **"with some background on solicitation and
  facilitation,"** instead of addressing any of the terms in the
  encouragement provision itself.[7]

14.3 Use a single quotation mark for a quote within another quote.

Quoting can get complicated, especially when the writer quotes one
source that's quoting another. In that case, use a double quotation
mark on the outside of the quotation and single quotation marks
within. In this next example, Justice Ginsburg quoted *Williams*, which
quoted the phrases "strong medicine" and "casually employed" from
another case.

- Nevermind that Sineneng-Smith's counsel had presented a
  contrary theory of the case in the District Court, and that this
  Court has repeatedly warned that **"invalidation** for [First
  Amendment] overbreadth is **'strong medicine'** that is not to be
  'casually employed.'" *United States* v. *Williams*, 553 U.S. 285,
  293 (2008) (quoting *Los Angeles Police Dept.* v. *United Reporting
  Publishing Corp.*, 528 U.S. 32, 39 (1999)).[8]

14.4 For a quote within a quote within yet another quote, switch between double and single quotation marks.

Yes, this happens. In the exceptionally rare case when the writer
quotes one source that's quoting another that's quoting yet another,
use a double quotation mark, then a single, then another double.

Follow the justices' lead here in invoking that triple usage rarely: triple quotes appeared only 46 times in five recent years. The last set of marks in the next example shows that triple use—for a quote within a quote within a quote.

- Flowers' counsel stated that when Flowers' father "'"was working as a greeter at Wal-Mart,"'" there was "'"probably not a person in Winona who wouldn't have said, "Mr. Archie's my friend."'"'[9]

14.5 For the rare block quote, use double indents and double quotation marks.

Block quotations (traditionally 50 words or more) are rare. You won't find one in most opinions. But when they appear, the justices do not follow the traditional *Bluebook* rule of leaving off the quotation marks.[10] In the next example here, Justice Kagan uses quotation marks around a block quote of Justice Joseph Story.

- Our seminal opinion on fair use quoted the illustrious Justice Story:

  "In truth, in literature, in science and in art, there are, and can be, few, if any, things, which . . . are strictly new and original throughout. Every book in literature, science and art, borrows, and must necessarily borrow, and use much which was well known and used before."[11]

Because the block quote format breaks up the page, the justices typically prefer quoting shorter phrases and passages, reserving the block format only for the especially memorable or necessary. Justice Breyer shows the short and long types here, with a block quote of a solicitor's speech from 1760, set up with one partial quote.

- Likewise, in the case of *Rex v. Lord Ferrers*, the solicitor general instructed the members of the House of Lords to consider the **"'capacity and intention'"** of the accused, to be sure, but what did he mean by those terms? The ultimate question of insanity, he explained, depended on the defendant's capacity at the time of the offense to distinguish right from wrong:

"My lords, the question therefore must be asked; is the noble prisoner at the bar to be acquitted from the guilt of murder, on account of insanity? It is not pretended to be a constant general insanity. Was he under the power of it, at the time of the offence committed? Could he, did he, at that time, distinguish between good and evil?"[12]

See related topics:

Brackets in Chapter 2
Colons in Chapter 3
Ellipses in Chapter 5
Exclamation Marks in Chapter 9
Question Marks in Chapter 13
Semicolons in Chapter 15

14.6 Unanimous rule: Always put periods and commas inside quotation marks; put larger punctuation marks (colons, exclamation points, question marks, and semicolons) inside *only* if part of the quote.

An easy way to remember this quotation-mark rule is to separate punctuation marks into two types: big and little. Periods and commas with their single dot and single swoosh, are tiny enough to always fit within the quotation marks. Bigger marks—colons, exclamation points, question marks, and semicolons—each have two parts (for example, two dots for a colon, a dot and a swoosh for a semicolon). These bigger marks fit inside the quotation marks only if part of the original.

14.6.1 Unanimous rule: Commas and periods always belong inside quotation marks.

- By the Government's own account, the traffic study the defendants used for a cover story was a **"sham,"** and they never asked to see its results.[13]
- As Kelly's own lawyer acknowledged, this case involves an **"abuse of power."**[14]

14.6.2 Unanimous rule: Colons, exclamation points, question marks, and semicolons belong inside quotation marks only when part of a quoted text.

- Title VII's message is **"simple but momentous"**: An individual employee's sex is "not relevant to the selection, evaluation, or compensation of employees."[15]
- Instead, the defendants argued that both of the laws under which they were punished really derived from the **"same sovereign:"** the national government, by way of the Eighteenth Amendment that authorized Prohibition.[16]
  - *Justice Gorsuch adds the colon to his sentence in the first example and quotes the colon in the second.*
- Why bother with a trial if "the finality of any judgment rendered by [a] Court will be **dubious"?**[17]
  - *Gorsuch quotes an order within his question.*
- At the start of its opinion, the majority asks this rhetorical question: "Why do Louisiana and Oregon allow nonunanimous **convictions?"**[18]
  - *Justice Alito quotes a question from the majority opinion.*
- Rather, we concluded that Congress enacted the FDCA "to bolster consumer protection against harmful **products;"** that

Congress provided no "*federal* remedy for consumers harmed by unsafe or ineffective **drugs**"; that Congress was "awar[e] of the prevalence of state tort **litigation;**" and that, whether Congress' general purpose was to protect consumers, to provide safety-related incentives to manufacturers, or both, language, history, and purpose all indicate that "Congress did not intend FDA oversight to be the exclusive means of ensuring drug safety and effectiveness."[19]

∘ *Only the first and third semicolons contained within this sentence are part of the case Breyer quotes here.*

15

Semicolons

The messages are often identical even down to commas and semicolons.[1]

—Justice William O. Douglas

15.1 Unanimous rule: Use a semicolon to offset items in a complex series or string citation, and on occasion, to combine two sentences into one.

"First rule: Do not use semicolons," Kurt Vonnegut advised in *A Man Without a Country*. "All they do is show you've been to college."[2] The justices have been to college and then some, but they don't abide by this idea. All nine use semicolons to combine complicated lists, citations, and sentences.

The semicolon takes the formal colon and the casual comma and creates a hybrid. It offers another way to break up a sentence or a series. One story places its birth in Venice in 1494, at a time of punctuation "tinkering" and "writerly experimentation and invention."[3] This combo of a swoosh and a dot lends clarity to writers' amalgamations. Just don't carry this sentence combiner too far. All the justices use semicolons to connect two sentences, but infrequently. (See Chapter 29, Short Words—and Sentences.)

The Supreme Guide to Writing. Jill Barton, Oxford University Press. © Oxford University Press 2024.
DOI: 10.1093/oso/9780197754351.003.0015

15.2 Unanimous rule: Use a semicolon to offset items in a complex series.

One common use for semicolons is separating items in a complicated list. That is, a list with items containing commas within or especially lengthy clauses. The serial semicolon separates items in the same way as a serial comma. It helps the writer avoid a messy soup of commas or a confusing sequence. Consider how muddled the next list would be if Chief Justice Roberts used commas, instead of semicolons, to separate the four clauses:

- Although the parties agree that this particular controversy is justiciable, we recognize **that** it is the first of its kind to reach this Court**; that** disputes of this sort can raise important issues concerning relations between the branches**; that** related disputes involving congressional efforts to seek official Executive Branch information recur on a regular basis, including in the context of deeply partisan controversy**; and that** Congress and the Executive have nonetheless managed for over two centuries to resolve such disputes among themselves without the benefit of guidance from us.[4]

The same rule applies to complex lists without commas. Justice Sotomayor uses semicolons for clarity here because the second item in the list contains two relative clauses beginning with *that*.

- Missing from the Court's opinion is any recognition **that** Congress found private enforcement suits and fiduciary duties critical to policing retirement plans**; that** it was after this litigation was initiated **that** respondents restored $311 million to the plan in compliance with statutorily required funding levels**; and that** counsel justified their fee request as a below-market percentage of the $311 million employer infusion that this lawsuit allegedly precipitated.[5]

And here, Sotomayor adds numbers for added clarity.

- The panel then held that "defense preclusion" bars a party from raising a defense where: "**(i)** a previous action involved an adjudication on the merits"; "**(ii)** the previous action involved the same parties"; "**(iii)** the defense was either asserted or could have been asserted, in the prior action"; **and** "**(iv)** the district court, in its discretion, concludes that preclusion of the defense is appropriate."[6]

15.3 Unanimous rule: Use a semicolon to combine two or more sentences into one.

When sentences are closely related, writers can combine them with a semicolon, instead of separating them into two (or more) sentences with a period. All the justices use this trick, but not in every opinion they write. Shorter sentences usually do the job better than longer ones. Here's how it's done:

- An ambulance struggled to reach the victim of a heart attack; police had trouble responding to a report of a missing child.[7]
- But a pair of jurors believed that the State of Louisiana had failed to prove Mr. Ramos's guilt beyond reasonable doubt; they voted to acquit.[8]
- (Like the courts below, we shall refer to the two doctors in the first case as Doe 1 and Doe 2; we shall refer to the two doctors in the second case as Doe 5 and Doe 6; and we shall refer to two other doctors then practicing in Louisiana as Doe 3 and Doe 4.)[9]

15.4 Unanimous rule: Use a semicolon and a comma to combine two sentences into one when using a long conjunction.

When a writer wants to combine two sentences and show how they are related, a longer conjunction, called a conjunctive adverb, can do the job. Unlike the tiny coordinating conjunctions of *and, but, or, so,* and *yet,* many conjunctive adverbs are three syllables or more. Common ones include *accordingly, consequently, furthermore, however, instead, moreover, nevertheless, nonetheless, otherwise, similarly, therefore,* and *thus.*

It's perhaps because of this innate complexity that conjunctive adverbs need a semicolon and a comma when they combine a sentence. And maybe because of that complexity, the justices hardly use this construction (for some, it's just once or twice in five years). The conjunction *but* appears 10,495 times in five years, but *however* appears only 1,525. (See Chapter 20 for more on conjunctions.) Here are a few of the rare examples:

- Federally recognized tribes undeniably fit that description; **therefore,** the Code's abrogation provision plainly applies to them as well.[10]
- So Hewitt was not exempt from the FLSA; **instead,** he was eligible under that statute for overtime pay.[11]
- First, the annotations are not created contemporaneously with the statutes to which they pertain; **instead,** the annotations comment on statutes already enacted.[12]
- If reopening is granted, any revision the Board makes may be reviewed in the same manner as a primary determination of benefits; **otherwise,** the revision is "binding."[13]

15.5 Unanimous rule: Use a semicolon to separate citations within a string cite.

Even though the justices rarely combine sentences with a semicolon, the swoosh-plus-dot appears on nearly every page of Court opinions—in citations. Semicolons separate string cites, short and long. The rule here is to list the newest and highest authorities first.

- We call that practice *Auer* deference, or sometimes *Seminole Rock* deference, after two cases in which we employed it. See *Auer* v. *Robbins*, 519 U.S. 452 (1997); *Bowles v. Seminole Rock & Sand Co.*, 325 U.S. 410 (1945).[14]
- To be "potentially responsible" for something meant then, as it does today, that a person could *possibly* be held accountable for it; the outcome is *capable of* happening. American Heritage Dictionary 1025 (1981); Webster's New Collegiate Dictionary 893 (1980).[15]
- We have long permitted abortion providers to invoke the rights of their actual or potential patients in challenges to abortion-related regulations. See, *e.g.*, *Whole Woman's Health*, 579 U.S., at ___ ; *Gonzales*, 550 U.S., at 133; *Ayotte v. Planned Parenthood of Northern New Eng.*, 546 U.S. 320, 324 (2006); *Stenberg v. Carhart*, 530 U.S. 914, 922 (2000); *Mazurek v. Armstrong*, 520 U.S. 968, 969–70 (1997) (*per curiam*); *Casey*, 505 U.S., at 845 (majority opinion); *Akron v. Akron Center for Reproductive Health, Inc.*, 462 U.S. 416, 440, n.30 (1983); *Planned Parenthood of Central Mo. v. Danforth*, 428 U.S. 52, 62 (1976); *Doe v. Bolton*, 410 U.S. 179, 188–89 (1973).[16]

16

Spaces

Freedoms of expression require "breathing space."[1]

—Justice Sandra Day O'Connor

16.1 Unanimous rule: Use an em-space after sentences.

This final punctuation debate has divided and vexed writers for decades. One space or two after a period? If you gave either answer, you're running afoul of the Court's standard. For published opinions in United States Reports, the justices use an em-space after each sentence.[2] That's just an extra-large space, like an em-dash is an extra-large dash. In typography, it's a space the size of a capital M.

So the Court might just appease everyone (or maybe no one) with its unanimous ruling on this one. If you want to follow the Court's lead, you can find the em-space, along with the em-dash and hyphen, in Microsoft Word. For the em-space, click "Insert Symbol," then "More Symbols," and then the "Special Characters" tab. A find-and-replace after a final edit could make the switch easier.

But if it's too much trouble to figure out how to type an extra-large space after each sentence, then just keep it simple and stick with one.

The Supreme Guide to Writing. Jill Barton, Oxford University Press. © Oxford University Press 2024.
DOI: 10.1093/oso/9780197754351.003.0016

PART II

Words

Language is the central tool of our trade.[1]

—Chief Justice John Roberts

Some writers mistakenly think it's more lawyerly to use big words, like *nevertheless* and *hitherto*. And some writers mistakenly follow outdated grammar advice and avoid starting sentences with *since, because, but*, and other conjunctions. And some—mistakenly, yes—shun double negatives, qualifiers, split infinitives, and prepositions at the end of sentences.

But the Supreme Court's greatest writers don't get these points wrong. They achieve a level of analytic precision, twisting their words around complicated language in a way that's plain and sensible. It's why, as Justice Kagan said, "the Chief is incapable of writing a bad sentence."

Kagan, who's also a writing virtuoso, went on to say that Chief Justice Roberts' writing "has deep intelligence, crystal clarity, grace, humor, and understated style," and that he has an "ability to see and organize and make lucid whole areas of law. His ability to explain—not only to lawyers, but to a wider public what his decisions are based on. Those qualities, they're more than craft. They're the foundation stones of the rule of law."[2]

The foundation for a lawyer's word choice is detailed in this section, charting the course so you too will never write a bad sentence.

17

Adjectives and Adverbs

But the adjectives are by far the best part of that response.[1]

—Justice Elena Kagan

17.1 Unanimous rule: Cut all unnecessary adjectives and adverbs.

Mark Twain advised writers to "kill" the adjectives and adverbs in their writing. But as with many writing rules, he qualified: "I don't mean utterly, but kill most of them—then the rest will be valuable. They weaken when they are close together. They give strength when they are wide apart."[2]

The justices unanimously follow a similar philosophy. When recounting the facts of a case or setting forth their analyses, the justices strip needless flourishes. They devote only about 5% of their words to adjectives and 3% to adverbs.[3]

But they can't "kill" all these auxiliary descriptors. The precise nature of the law requires elucidation. The crime of murder, for instance, is not just a "killing" but the "intentional killing of a human being." The definition requires the specificity from the adjective "intentional" to differentiate it from an accidental killing, a legal distinction judges and juries must often make.[4]

Plenty of cases turn on how the justices interpret an adjective,[5] adverb,[6] or longer descriptive clauses.[7] Chief Justice Roberts explained "the ordinary understanding of how adjectives work" in breaking down the term "critical habitat" for endangered species (where "critical" is the adjective and "habitat" is the noun).

The Supreme Guide to Writing. Jill Barton, Oxford University Press. © Oxford University Press 2024.
DOI: 10.1093/oso/9780197754351.003.0017

"Adjectives modify nouns—they pick out a subset of a category that possesses a certain quality," Roberts wrote. "It follows that 'critical habitat' is the subset of 'habitat' that is 'critical' to the conservation of an endangered species."[8]

Just as some nouns need modifiers, so too do verbs. The law must differentiate between a person who "accidentally" dispenses a controlled substance and a defendant who "knowingly or intentionally" does so. Justice Breyer explains that it's essential to apply the adverbs "knowingly or intentionally" there to separate "wrongful from innocent acts."[9]

Cases revolving around adjective or adverb questions typically focus on how the descriptive term or phrase affects the noun or verb it's meant to modify. For instance, one tech giant argued that the adjective "full" before the word "costs" in the Copyright Act authorized courts to award expenses beyond those specified. The Court unanimously disagreed, with Justice Kavanaugh helpfully explaining:

- The adjective "full" in §505 therefore does not alter the meaning of the word "costs." Rather, "full costs" are all the "costs" otherwise available under law. The word "full" operates in the phrase "full costs" just as it operates in other common phrases: A "full moon" means the moon, not Mars. A "full breakfast" means breakfast, not lunch. A "full season ticket plan" means tickets, not hot dogs. So too, the term "full costs" means *costs*, not other expenses.[10]

Adverbs affect verbs in the same way adjectives affect nouns. The descriptors modify or qualify a term or phrase. They can express a relation of cause or circumstance, time or place, or manner or degree. But they do not change the intrinsic meaning of the modified term, as with the phrase "obtained, directly or indirectly." Justice Sotomayor explains:

- The adverbs "directly" and "indirectly" modify—but do not erase—the verb "obtain." In other words, these adverbs refer to how a defendant obtains the property; they do not negate the requirement that he obtain it at all. For instance, the marijuana mastermind might receive payments directly from drug purchasers, or he might arrange to have drug purchasers pay an intermediary such as the college student. In all instances, he ultimately "obtains" the property—whether "directly or indirectly."[11]

The takeaway—from a grammatical perspective—is for legal writers to consider how descriptors affect the words or phrases they modify. The takeaway—from a stylistic perspective—is for legal writers to use adjectives and adverbs sparingly. And to make sure they add meaning. As Justice Kagan complained in a dissent: "If, as today's majority says, *Teague* is full of 'adjectives,' so too is *Ramos*—and mostly the same ones."[12]

Roberts masters the art of peppering a story with a few adjectives and adverbs to bring it to life. In a case involving an endangered frog, he chooses only the necessary adjectives to paint a picture of its unusual defense mechanisms, "plump" body, and "dark," "dusky" coloring and spots. He then depicts where the frogs live. The details show Roberts considered the creature and its specific habitat before issuing a unanimous ruling against it.

- The amphibian *Rana sevosa* is popularly known as the "dusky gopher frog"—"**dusky**" because of its **dark** coloring and "**gopher**" because it lives underground. The dusky gopher frog is **about three inches long**, with a **large** head, **plump** body, and **short** legs. Warts dot its back, and **dark** spots cover its **entire** body. It is noted for covering its eyes with its **front** legs when it feels threatened, peeking out periodically until danger passes. Less endearingly, it also secretes a **bitter, milky** substance to deter **would-be** diners.

  The frog spends **most of its** time in burrows and **stump** holes located in **upland longleaf pine** forests. In **such** forests, **frequent** fires help maintain an **open** canopy, which in turn allows vegetation to grow on the **forest** floor. The vegetation supports the **small** insects that the frog eats and provides a place for the frog's eggs to attach when it breeds. The frog breeds in "**ephemeral**" ponds that are dry for part of the year. **Such** ponds are safe for tadpoles because **predatory** fish cannot live in them.[13]

Alongside these adjectives, Roberts blends in descriptors for his verbs to add depth and clarity, but without too many trimmings. Here, the passage is again, with the adverbs bolded.

- The amphibian *Rana sevosa* is **popularly** known as the "dusky gopher frog"—"dusky" because of its dark coloring and "gopher" because it lives **underground**. The dusky gopher frog is about three inches long, with a large head, plump body, and short legs. Warts dot its back, and dark spots cover its entire body. It is noted for covering its eyes with its front legs when it feels threatened, peeking out **periodically until danger passes. Less endearingly**, it also secretes a bitter, milky substance to deter would-be diners.[14]

The here-and-there bolding in these paragraphs shows Roberts uses adjectives and adverbs to deepen a story, not to distract. They are essential to the story but secondary to the main players and issues—both in the opinion and in each sentence, where the main players are the subjects and verbs.

In fact, Roberts previously chastised a judge for adding such descriptors to dodge a difficult issue, stating, "it is not enough to repeat the analysis of the merits decision, and add adjectives."[15] He's also described debating particularly unforgiving adjectives in dissents with his colleagues. "Sometimes . . . the dissent is saying pretty harsh things. As you all know, some of those harsh things see the light of day. But you know, you should see some that didn't," he said with a laugh. "And that's when you know, you sort of represent the Court in talking to one of your colleagues and saying, 'We understand that you think that this is important, and we understand that you think it's wrong, but this particular adjective is not the one to use.'"[16]

Good writers use adjectives and adverbs deliberately, not haphazardly. Note how these sentences would lose their meaning if the adjectives or adverbs were cut.

• The federal government had **darker** designs.[17]
• The United States offers up a **rapacious** interpretation . . . .[18]
• In the century that followed, however, the Amendment proved
  little more than a **parchment** promise.[19]
• The Court **incorrectly** suggests that the Government's position
  will sweep in foreign defendants with only a minimal connection
  to the United States.[20]
• Speculating about what this Court might have thought about
  arguments it never addressed **needlessly** introduces confusion.
  This Court looks for definitive interpretations, not holdings in
  hiding.[21]

With a smattering of adjectives and adverbs, the justices show the
truth in Twain's advice, that "they give strength when they are wide
apart."[22] As Kagan noted in one dissent, judges can't be averse to adjectives and adverbs when they are searching for truth: "No wonder
today's majority declares a new-found aversion to 'adjectives'—or, as
a concurring opinion says, 'all these words,'" Kagan wrote, arguing for
unanimity in criminal jury verdicts. "For only then is the jury's finding
of guilt certain enough—secure enough, mistake-proof enough—to
take away the person's freedom."[23]

18

Alliteration and Repetition

Other cases of ours have repeated that language.[1]

—Chief Justice John Roberts

18.1 Unanimous guiding principle: Put your best points on repeat.

Justice Gorsuch is among the most entertaining writers on the Court, but his critics faulted him for overdoing the alliteration in his first opinion: "Disruptive dinnertime calls, downright deceit, and more besides drew Congress's eye to the debt collection industry."[2]

Gorsuch's attempts to stylize his writing during his first year on the Court earned him criticism and the mocking hashtag #GorsuchStyle on Twitter (the social media site now known as X).[3] Legal writing experts (including this one) found the derision misplaced, and it soon faded.

Gorsuch has since regained the reputation he earned on the U.S. Court of Appeals as a "brilliant," "playful," and "witty" writer,[4] as the more understated examples on the next few pages illustrate. Perhaps more than his colleagues, he takes advantage of poetic devices, such as alliteration, assonance, consonance, and repetition.[5] These literary tools make lines flow more smoothly and memorably, as this poem that Justice Alito borrowed shows, by employing all the above:

> In Flanders fields the poppies blow
> Between the crosses, row on row.[6]

The Supreme Guide to Writing. Jill Barton, Oxford University Press. © Oxford University Press 2024.
DOI: 10.1093/oso/9780197754351.003.0018

18.2 Unanimous rule: Use occasional alliteration, assonance, and consonance for emphasis, flow, and memorability.

Good writing has a rhythm, just like good music. Readers, in a sense, hear the words they see as their eyes move down the page, so repeated sounds make the lines stand out because they are more lyrical. All the justices use a touch of alliteration, assonance, and consonance in their writing to infuse a beat into their sentences.

Alliteration is the repetition of sounds at the start of words, as with the *d* sounds in "Disruptive dinnertime calls, downright deceit . . . ." Assonance is the repetition of vowel sounds, as with the short *i* sounds in *disruptive* and *dinnertime*. Consonance is the repetition of consonants.

The trick is keeping it subtle, not jumping off the page but nearly imperceptibly compelling the reader onward. These next sentences show the restrained art of alliteration by Gorsuch (as promised).

- Recognizing as much, the **Court** today **cuts** through the **kudzu**.[7]
- To my mind, three **contextual clues confirm** that this reading of the statutory text is the **correct** one.[8]
- Today, the Court rejects a request the **Navajo Nation never** made.[9]

The justices also sprinkle in the less perceptible rhythmic tools of assonance and consonance. Justice Kagan gives a dusting of all three tools in this next sentence.

- And that kind of **message matters** in **assessing confusion** because **consumers** are not so likely to think that the **maker** of a **mocked product** is itself doing the **mocking**.[10]

First, there's alliteration with the repetition of the same letter or sound at the start of words: *confusion* and *consumers*, along with the quintuple hit of *message, matters, maker, mocked,* and *mocking*.

Second, there's assonance with the middle *oo* syllables of *confusion* (kuhn·**fyoo**·zhn) and *consumers* (kuhn·**soo**·mrs). And finally, there's consonance with the *-ess* sound in *message* and *assessing* and the *-kt* sound ending *mocked* and *product*. Breaking down literary tools like this diminishes the effect. That's why good writers don't use them in a hit-you-over-the-head obvious way, but instead delicately scatter them throughout their writing.

Alliteration, assonance, and consonance can make phrases stick with you. Chief Justice Roberts used the phrase "reticulated remedial regime" in a 2005 lower court opinion.[11] Alito repeated it in 2023.[12] In between, nine other courts copied the phrase, almost lifting the triple alliterative to a legal term of art.

18.3 Unanimous rule: Repeated elements make lines memorable.

When used well, repetition creates a memorable melody. All nine justices take advantage of this persuasive tool. The human brain likes patterns, especially groups of three, because they create an attractive, familiar rhythm.[13] These examples show how the justices draw the reader in by repeating the exact same words and phrases.

- Here is a fact of the matter: Congress delegates to agencies often and broadly. And it usually does so for sound reasons. **Because** agencies have expertise Congress lacks. **Because** times and circumstances change, and agencies are better able to keep up and respond. **Because** Congress knows that if it had to do everything, many desirable and even necessary things wouldn't get done.[14]
- **They fail** to cite *Hunt*. **They fail** to cite *Croson*. **They fail** to mention that the entirety of their analysis of the Equal Protection Clause—the statistics, the cases, the history—has been considered and rejected before.[15]
- Understanding this lawsuit requires at least three pieces of context the Court's opinion neglects. **It requires** some understanding of

the history that led to the Treaty of 1868 establishing the Navajo Reservation. **It requires** some insight into the discussions that surrounded that Treaty. Finally, **it requires** an appreciation of the many steps the Navajo took to avoid this litigation.[16]

- **Everyone agrees** the Navajo received enforceable water rights by treaty. **Everyone agrees** the United States holds some of those water rights in trust on the Tribe's behalf. And **everyone agrees** the extent of those rights has never been assessed.[17]

Matching phrases are melodic, even when in groups of two or four. Or when more subtle, as in the next examples.

- The Tribe was forced to rely on a "'little stream winding through an immense plain." But its "water was bad." **No surprise**, then, that "[o]nly half the land under cultivation at the Bosque was productive." **No surprise** either that even the productive land yielded "one disastrous crop failure after another."[18]
- **Arriving** at that conclusion proved simple enough; **arriving** upon a treaty proved more challenging.[19]
- By now, the reason why should be obvious. . . . It **will stifle** creativity of every sort. It **will impede** new art and music and literature. It **will thwart** the expression of new ideas and the attainment of new knowledge. It **will make** our world poorer.[20]
- That is a **remarkable** view of the judicial role—**remarkably** wrong. Lost in the false pretense of judicial humility that the dissent espouses is a claim to power **so radical**, **so destructive**, that it required a Second Founding to undo.[21]
- Odd that a book about **pirates** should have practiced **piracy**?[22]

18.4 Unanimous rule: Repeated elements must be parallel and match in grammatical form.

Repetition doesn't always mean matching exactly. When the justices take advantage of this rhetorical move in a more general sense, they ensure their repeated elements are parallel—or matching in grammatical structure. That means when one element in a series begins with a noun, preposition, or a subject-verb clause, they all do. And when the first element of a series contains a verb, all verbs match in tense. It doesn't just read better that way; it's good grammar. Strong verbs here help carry Roberts' and Gorsuch's points.

- Courts will puzzle over whether an officer exercises control when he **grabs** a suspect, when he **tackles** him, or only when he **slaps** on the cuffs.[23]
- Common law courts never said the same of bailiffs who **fired** arrows at debtors, **shot** them with firearms, or **cudgeled** them as they ran away.[24]
- Players **press** a button, graphics **spin**, noise **plays**, and eventually players **learn** whether they have won or lost.[25]
- The Navajo have tried it all. They **have written** federal officials. They **have moved** this Court to clarify the United States' responsibilities when representing them. They **have sought to intervene** directly in water-related litigation.[26]

Nouns in a series don't have to be all singular or plural, but a series flows nicely when they are:

- The route to obtaining collateral relief is presently replete with **imagined artificial barriers**, **arbitrary dead ends**, and **traps for the unwary**.[27]
- Laws dividing **parks and golf courses; neighborhoods and businesses; buses and trains; schools and juries** were undone, all by a transformative promise "stemming from our American ideal . . . ."[28]
- These stories are not **every student's story**. But they are **many students' stories**.[29]

19

Because vs. Since

But words are how the law constrains power.[1]

—Justice Neil Gorsuch

19.1 Unanimous guiding principle: Start sentences with *because* or *since* and consider the precise meaning of each when using one in a sentence.

"Because of sex" became one of the most important phrases of the 2019 term. In a landmark case, Justice Gorsuch wrote that when federal law prohibits employment discrimination "because of sex," it prohibits discrimination based on sexual orientation and gender identity.

"For an employer to discriminate against employees for being homosexual or transgender, the employer must intentionally discriminate against individual men and women in part because of sex," Gorsuch wrote. "That has always been prohibited by Title VII's plain terms—and that 'should be the end of the analysis.'"[2]

Gorsuch's textualist approach was one reason behind the ruling, and it also might be why he carefully uses the words *because* and *since* throughout his opinions in the traditional sense. Grammarians have insisted that *since*, which technically means "from the time that," should be used to show only a temporal relation.[3] Meanwhile, *because*, defined as "for the reason that,"[4] should show only cause.

That distinction is often lost in everyday conversation. In fact, eight of the justices use *since* to mean *because* during oral arguments, but only a very slim majority has done so in a written opinion—and

The Supreme Guide to Writing. Jill Barton, Oxford University Press. © Oxford University Press 2024.
DOI: 10.1093/oso/9780197754351.003.0019

rarely at that.[5] They also unanimously ignore the common misconception that writers shouldn't start sentences with *because* or *since*.

19.2 The super-slim majority rule: Use *since* interchangeably with *because* rarely and only when the meaning is clear.

The distinction between *since* and *because* typically matters only when confusion would result. Consider the sentence, "Since she went to the meeting on Monday, the witness had second thoughts about testifying." The reader doesn't know if the witness reconsidered testifying because of the meeting or at some point after the meeting, perhaps for another reason.

Some legal writing gurus urge that the distinction between *because* (showing cause) and *since* (showing time) is more important in legal writing. After all, causation is the root of many disputes. The justices are split on the question, swapping *because* for *since* very rarely and only when the meaning is unmistakable. Justices Kagan, Kavanaugh, and Barrett have never done so; Justices Sotomayor and Gorsuch have swapped *because* for *since* only once in five years.[6]

Legal writing demands precision. That helps explain why the justices use *because* eight times more than the ambiguous *since* (5,939 versus 735 times in five terms). Very few of those *since* references mean *because*. Here, Chief Justice Roberts shows how to use *since* to show cause—and only where readers wouldn't confuse the meaning:

- Washington's request must have struck him as reasonable enough, **since** English sovereigns regularly sought advice from their courts.[7]
- **Since** this was the first such request from Congress, President Washington called a Cabinet meeting, wishing to take care that his response "be rightly conducted" because it could "become a precedent."[8]

Still, keep in mind the tight split here. Nearly all the justices' references to *since* describe timing, as opposed to cause.

- And **since** our decisions in *Hartman* and *Reichle*, no court of appeals has applied that approach in retaliatory arrest cases of this sort.[9]
- Because of its sacred meaning, the Latin cross has been used to mark Christian deaths **since** at least the fourth century.[10]

19.3 Unanimous rule: Start sentences with *since* or *because.*

All the justices shun the antiquated grammar myth that *since* and *because* shouldn't start sentences. That non-rule could stem from grammar teachers who tell students not to start sentences this way in hopes of avoiding sentence fragments.[11] But the justices know better:

- **Since** we are not required to attempt an answer in this case, the prudent course is to hold back.[12]
- **Since** due process provided an independent ground for the decision below **and since** respondent urges us to affirm on this ground, it is hard to understand the dissent's argument that the due process issue was not "seriously in dispute below" or that it is somehow improper for us to decide the issue.[13]
- **Because** he succeeded in making it 25 yards into U.S. territory before he was caught, he claims the right to be treated more favorably.[14]
- **Because** the Government cannot meet that burden, Barton should prevail.[15]

Collectively, the justices have started 1,158 sentences in five years with *because* or *since.* And here, Kagan flouts that old grammar myth, intentionally creating fragments beginning with *because.*

- If a single statute represents the best of America, it is the Voting Rights Act. . . . If a single statute reminds us of the worst of America, it is the Voting Rights Act. **Because** it was—and remains—so necessary. **Because** a century after the Civil War was fought, at the time of the Act's passage, the promise of political equality remained a distant dream for African American citizens. **Because** States and localities continually "contriv[ed] new rules," mostly neutral on their face but discriminatory in operation, to keep minority voters from the polls. **Because** "Congress had reason to suppose" that States would "try similar maneuvers in the future"—"pour[ing] old poison into new bottles" to suppress minority votes. **Because** Congress has been proved right.[16]

20

Conjunctions

In particular, the majority zeros in on the disjunctive conjunction "or,"
and proceeds to build its entire opinion around that linguistic feature.[1]

—Justice Neil Gorsuch

20.1 Unanimous guiding principle: Start sentences with conjunctions, and choose *and*, *but*, *or*, *so*, and *yet* over their longer cousins.

Writing style choices can stir debate, and one of the more famous disputes was between two greats: William Faulkner and Ernest Hemingway. Faulkner accused Hemingway of lacking courage because he never used words "that might send the reader to the dictionary." Hemingway's retort: "Poor Faulkner. Does he really think big emotions come from big words? He thinks I don't know the ten-dollar words. I know them all right. But there are older and simpler and better words, and those are the ones I use."[2]

The justices habitually follow Hemingway's lead. As Justice Thomas once advised, "the genius is not to write a five-cent idea in a ten-dollar sentence. It's to put a ten-dollar idea in a five-cent sentence."[3]

The goal is to achieve clarity and simplicity without losing meaning. "That doesn't mean that there's no law in it," Thomas continued. "But there are simple ways to put important things in language that's accessible."[4]

The Supreme Guide to Writing. Jill Barton, Oxford University Press. © Oxford University Press 2024.
DOI: 10.1093/oso/9780197754351.003.0020

20.2 Unanimous rule: Use conjunctions, preferably the short ones, to start sentences.

One way the justices create these five-cent sentences is by starting them with short, punchy conjunctions. All nine sprinkle their opinions with sentences opening with *and*, *but*, *or*, *so*, and *yet*. And they opt for these short sentence starters significantly more than longer conjunctions, such as *however* and *nevertheless*. Take, for example, Justice Kagan's simple quips:

- **And** that is only the half of it.[5]
- **But** that argument gets things backwards.[6]
- **Or**, because he did not know his conduct broke the law. **Or**, because he could not control his behavior. **Or**, because of anything else.[7]
- **So** there is no doubt what Congress meant to accomplish.[8]
- **Yet** one more land dispute loomed.[9]

To help prove this point, here she uses three in a row:

- **So** there is naturally a section in the immigration laws that specifies how that process works. **But** nothing in §1184 (or any other section) states that admission is a prerequisite of nonimmigrant status—or otherwise said, that the former is a necessary incident of the latter. **And** that is what Sanchez needs.[10]

Even so, the myth that writers should avoid using these tiny conjunctions to start sentences persists.[11] The criticism for *so* is particularly intense. Some writers argue that *so* should be shunned—that it's akin to using *well*, *um*, and *like*, that it's a crutch puffing up language and undermining the writer's credibility.[12] In speech, *so* can indicate a verbal tic as much as a transition or connection.

But in Supreme Court opinions, it works, and shows up frequently, here in the first opinions of Justices Gorsuch, Kavanaugh, and Barrett:

- **So** perhaps it comes as little surprise that we now face a question about who exactly qualifies as a "debt collector" subject to the Act's rigors.[13]
- **So** why waste the time and money?[14]
- **So** the Services shelved the draft opinions and agreed with the EPA to extend the period of consultation.[15]

In fact, in five recent years, the justices began 1,221 sentences with *so*—a noteworthy jump from just a few years ago.[16]

20.3 Unanimous rule: Favor the concise conjunction over the clunky conjunctive adverb, not just at a sentence's start.

Lawyers get a bad rap for choosing the esoteric over the easy. First-year law students love to write words like *hitherto* and *thereunto* to try to sound more lawyerly, but more experienced legal writers know to opt for unruffled language. That was evident in one of the early cases challenging the 2021 Texas abortion law, where parts of a judicial clerk's draft order were accidentally published, revealing a "whereby" and other wordy phrases cut from the judge's final version.[17]

Consider a common word like *however* versus its punchier counterpart, *but*. The justices used *but* seven times more than *however* in five recent years, with *but* appearing on every page, on average. They start sentences with *but* at least 1,000 times a term, while *however* has reached that same starting line only 72 times in five years.

And here's more proof: The justices used *yet* 856 times, compared to *nevertheless* (188 times) and *nonetheless* (216 times) in more than 10,000 pages. And they used the ever-popular *so* hundreds more times[18] than *accordingly* (349 times), *consequently* (98), *moreover* (438), and *whereby* (13 times with 6 of them in quotes). The takeaway: opt for the easy word nearly every chance you get.

Choose this	Not that
And	Additionally, In Addition
	Furthermore
	Moreover
But	However
	Nonetheless
	Nevertheless
Or	Alternatively
	Conversely
	Otherwise
So	Accordingly
	Consequently
	Subsequently
Yet	Hitherto
	In spite of that
	Thus far

21

Modifiers

Modification implies growth. It is the life of the law.[1]
—Justice Louis D. Brandeis

21.1 Unanimous guiding principle: Avoid confusion, typically by placing modifiers close to what they modify.

No grammar topic stands accused of sentence gymnastics more than the modifier. A modifier is any word, phrase, or clause that alters a sentence's meaning. Justice Kagan includes a few here:

- VIP is a dog toy company, making and selling a product line of chewable rubber toys that it calls "Silly Squeakers."[2]

The core sentence is: *VIP is a company*. Three modifiers limit the meaning: the adjective (or noun phrase) *dog toy*; the gerund phrase, *making and selling a product line of chewable rubber toys*; and the restrictive clause, *that it calls "Silly Squeakers."*

Trouble can arise when readers need to interpret what a modifying phrase in a sentence actually modifies. And three recent cases have turned on that precise question.[3] Only one resulted in a unanimous judgment, and even then, Justice Alito concurred to warn that "rigid" and "arcane" grammar rules "can lead us astray."[4]

In the second case, a dissenting Justice Gorsuch argued that the majority's two competing theories for interpreting a statute were unpersuasive, noting that a "clause that leaps over its nearest referent

The Supreme Guide to Writing. Jill Barton, Oxford University Press. © Oxford University Press 2024.
DOI: 10.1093/oso/9780197754351.003.0021

to modify every other term would defy grammatical gravity and common sense alike."[5]

The third modifier case, *Lockhart v. United States*, addressed the "rule of the last antecedent." If that sounds like grammar gibberish, the guiding principle here simplifies the matter: Use modifiers in a way that avoids confusion, typically by placing them close to what they modify.

The *Supreme Guide* rules vary from tradition here. While the justices follow the basic rule to avoid misplaced modifiers, they don't always avoid what grammarians call dangling or unclear modifiers, where a modifier's placement could technically carry multiple interpretations (what grammar nerds sometimes call a "squinting" modifier). When it comes to modifying words, phrases, and clauses, all nine justices push the limits to follow conversational conventions over timeworn grammar guidelines.

21.2 Unanimous rule: Avoid misplaced modifiers.

When moving a modifier changes the meaning of a sentence, the justices take care to place the modifier exactly where it needs to be. Commonly misplaced modifiers include descriptors, such as *almost*, *hardly*, *just*, *mainly*, *nearly*, *only*, *predominantly*, and *primarily*. When you move these modifiers around in a sentence, interpretations can change—causing mistakes every legal writer should avoid. Note how the meaning of this next example changes when shifting the word *only*.

- In a Nation governed by the rule of law, not men (or willful judges), **only** Congress may withdraw this Nation's treaty promises or revise its written laws.[6]
  - *This placement of "only" means Congress—and no other entity—can act.*

- In a Nation governed by the rule of law, not men (or willful judges), Congress **only** may withdraw this Nation's treaty promises or revise its written laws.
  - *This altered placement of "only" means Congress has just the one power, which is incorrect.*
- In a Nation governed by the rule of law, not men (or willful judges), Congress may withdraw **only** this Nation's treaty promises or revise its written laws.

  - *This altered placement of "only" means Congress has the power to withdraw this Nation's treaty promises but nothing else.*

Writers often drop single-word modifiers haphazardly into sentences, but mistaken meanings can occur with longer modifying phrases too.

- **At the time**, Andrew Beshear, a Democrat, served as Kentucky's attorney general.
  - *"At that time" means when Beshear was attorney general.*[7]
- Andrew Beshear, a Democrat **at the time**, served as Kentucky's attorney general.
  - *This altered placement of "at that time" misstates that Beshear switched parties.*

The solution is to keep the modifying word or phrase as close as possible to what it modifies (that's called the antecedent). When using multiple modifying phrases in a sentence, place them logically to make the meaning clear. In other words, place modifiers in a sentence exactly the way you would use them when speaking.

In the next example, the antecedent is *today's decision*—at the beginning of the sentence. It belongs with the modifying phrase beginning with *which*—at the very end of the sentence. Moving the antecedent and modifier closer would get in the way of the other modifying phrases: *to mandate*, *with schools*, and *that teach religion*. So Justice Sotomayor places all the modifiers in the most logical order.

- I do not understand today's decision **to** mandate **that** SAUs contract directly **with** schools **that** teach religion, which would go beyond *Zelman*'s private-choice doctrine and blatantly violate the Establishment Clause.[8]

Imagine how confusing the next sentence would be if Sotomayor mixed up any of the eight modifying phrases within. As she shows here, when writing complicated sentences, writers need to arrange multiple modifiers in a way that ensures their meaning is presented as intended.

- Fennell—waiving a prior invocation of the Fifth Amendment— testified that he and Stites had watched television together **on** the evening **of** April 22 **before** going **to** sleep, and that Stites had left **for** work **at** her usual time **around** 3 a.m. **on** April 23.[9]

21.3 Unanimous rule: Avoid dangling modifiers unless the meaning is unmistakable.

A modifier is left dangling if the person or thing it modifies (again, that's called the antecedent) is missing from the sentence. The dangling happens when the subject is swapped out for something that's not doing the action. Grammarians get out their red pens at the sight of a missing antecedent, and in some cases, they would help writers avoid embarrassing misreads. The justices don't dangle modifiers in this way, but to illustrate, here's one sentence, radically reworked to show how confusion can result:

- **Living and breeding in ponds** that are safe for tadpoles because predatory fish cannot live in them, **the U.S. Fish and Wildlife Service** designated four sites for the conservation of the gopher frog.[10]

While a careful reader might figure out the gopher frog is the intended subject of the sentence, this example reads as though the Fish and Wildlife Service is living and breeding in ponds, which obviously defies possibility.

In other instances of dangling modifiers, though, grammarians should cap their red pens. All nine justices dangle modifiers when their point is otherwise clear, just as many of us do in conversation. This swing at tradition shows that when first-rate writers get the basics right, they can bend hackneyed rules. In these next examples, Justices Thomas, Kagan, Alito, Gorsuch, Kavanaugh, Barrett, and Ginsburg, respectively, dangle their modifiers.

- **Having taken** that step, **one thing** is certain: This will not be the last time it is asked to do so.[11]
  - *The actor in both sentences is the Court, not the ambiguous "one thing."*
- **Applying** our longstanding precedent, **the answer** is clear: It does not.[12]
  - *The "answer" didn't apply anything, but it's clear the justices did.*
- **Taking** the provision's operative words in turn, **the term** "stay" is commonly used to describe an order that "suspend[s] judicial alteration of the status quo."[13]
  - *The "term" can't do any taking.*
- **Having invoked** these sundry considerations, **it's** hard to see how the majority might disown them.[14]
  - *The undefined pronoun "it" is not the actor.*
- **Having said** all that, **our point** here should not be read too broadly.[15]
  - *The majority has said much; the "point" is narrower than the intended subject.*
- **Considering** the record as a whole, **Florida** has not shown that it is "highly probable" that Georgia's alleged overconsumption played more than a trivial role in the collapse of Florida's oyster fisheries.[16]
  - *Florida isn't doing the considering; the Court is.*

- **Applying** *Atlantic Sounding*'s test, **punitive damages** are not categorically barred in unseaworthiness actions.[17]
  - *Punitive damages are not—and cannot—apply anything.*

But take note: the justices dangle a modifier rarely and only when the subject being modified is otherwise clear.[18] For example, if the modifier is clear in a previous sentence, the justices at times might skip it in other sentences. Note how Alito leaves the modifier dangling when he has made the subject clear in sentences before and after the alleged grammatical error.

- **We** begin by considering the critical question whether the Constitution, properly understood, confers a right to obtain an abortion. **Skipping over that question, the controlling opinion** in *Casey* reaffirmed *Roe*'s "central holding" based solely on the doctrine of stare decisis, but as **we** will explain, proper application of stare decisis required an assessment of the strength of the grounds on which *Roe* was based.
  - *The Court is the one skipping, not the Casey opinion.*

As in conversation, context matters. The justices always make the actor clear, within a few sentences, just as anyone would when speaking. In the next example, Gorsuch leaves a modifier dangling but makes the actor clear in the previous sentence.

- And **I** would have thought that restatement of the law more than enough to resolve today's case. **Having now effectively abandoned** *Granholm*'s distinction between products and their distribution and promising to subject both to dormant Commerce Clause scrutiny, **it's** hard not to wonder what's left of Webb-Kenyon and § 2.[19]

The subject "I" in the first sentence shows that Gorsuch is the subject who's wondering, along with the fact that it's his dissent.

21.4 Unanimous rule: Avoid unclear modifiers by considering context and common understanding.

In some cases, there is just one "ordinary understanding of how English works," as Kagan has assured.[20] For instance, in the David-versus-Goliath case of *Facebook, Inc. v. Duguid*, the justices unanimously agreed with the social media company's reading of a federal statute.

Noah Duguid sued Facebook for mistakenly and repeatedly sending him text messages using that abusive telemarketing invention called an "autodialer." The case hinged on interpreting the definition of the term, and specifically, these bolded parts:

"equipment which has the capacity—to **store** or **produce** telephone numbers to be called, **using a random or sequential number generator**; and to dial such numbers."[21]

Facebook's equipment did "store" and "dial" numbers, but not "using a random or sequential number generator." This is where the sentence gymnastics comes in. Duguid's attorney, the well-known lexicographer Bryan Garner, argued that the modifying phrase, "using a random or sequential number generator," modified only the verb closest to it, "produce," but not the other verb in the phrase, "store."

That reading would mean if equipment can simply "store" and "dial" numbers, as Facebook's equipment did, Duguid would prevail. In other words, the bolded portions shown in this next version (conveniently working in Duguid's favor) should be read together, while the rest can be ignored.

• equipment which has the capacity—**to store** or produce telephone numbers to be called, using a random or sequential number generator; **and to dial such numbers**.

So in other, other words, because Facebook's equipment did "store" and "dial" numbers, Duguid wins. The sentence manipulation is comparable the $2 million comma case (see Chapter 4), where one reading can essentially omit a nonrestrictive clause from a sentence.

But don't bet on it.[22] As Sotomayor wrote for a unanimous Court, there's "'no grammatical basis' for arbitrarily stretching the modifier back to include 'produce,' but not so far back as to include 'store.'"[23] In a concise 12 pages, Sotomayor also noted that the modifying clause "immediately follows a concise, integrated clause."[24]

In the concurrence, Alito shook up that simple understanding. He explained, "it is very easy to think of sentences that clearly go against the canon."[25] He offered a few obvious examples where the modifier at the end of the sentence modifies only the single term that immediately precedes it:

- When his owner comes home, the dog wags his tail and barks loudly.[26]
  - *The dog can't wag his tail loudly.*
- It is illegal to hunt rhinos and giraffes with necks longer than three feet.[27]
  - *Only giraffes have a long neck.*
- She likes to swim and run wearing track spikes.[28]
  - *Nobody swims wearing track spikes.*

Alito further explained that for some modifiers, our "understanding has little to do with syntax and everything to do with our common understanding."[29] That's why an old practice of doing a corpus linguistics analysis, or as Alito put it, "an analysis of how particular combinations of words are used in a vast database of English prose," doesn't work today.[30]

Instead, writers should focus on context and Kagan's common or "ordinary understanding of how English works." Consider that in conversation, lawyers can easily move modifying phrases around in a sentence—because context and inflection help impart meaning and because conversational conventions allow a more relaxed style.

That common, relaxed style should guide the placement of modifiers in writing too. In *Lockhart*, Kagan uses her renowned relaxed style to offer this easy explanation of modifiers. Her examples contradict Alito's dog and giraffe examples. But considering the context and common understanding, those contradictions make perfect sense:

> Imagine a friend told you that she hoped to meet "**an actor, director, or producer involved with the new Star Wars movie.**" You would know immediately that she wanted to meet an actor from the Star Wars cast—not an actor in, for example, the latest Zoolander. Suppose a real estate agent promised to find a client "**a house, condo, or apartment in New York.**" Wouldn't the potential buyer be annoyed if the agent sent him information about condos in Maryland or California? And consider a law imposing a penalty for the "**violation of any statute, rule, or regulation relating to insider trading.**" Surely a person would have cause to protest if punished under that provision for violating a traffic statute. The reason in all three cases is the same: Everyone understands that the modifying phrase—"**involved with the new Star Wars movie,**" "**in New York,**" "**relating to insider trading**"— applies to each term in the preceding list, not just the last.[31]

While Kagan's straightforward explanation comes from a dissent, even Sotomayor, who authored the majority opinions in all three recent modifier cases, agrees that common understanding should control. It's just that the statute at issue in *Lockhart* didn't comport with anyone's common understanding. The law's "inartful drafting" made for "odd repetition and inelegant phrasing," and it "is hardly the way an average person, or even an average lawyer, would set about to describe the relevant conduct."[32]

So with modifiers, that's exactly what writers should do here: Start from scratch. Consider the old rules, but discard them when conversational style (and sense) should come through instead. As Kagan put it in oral argument: "sometimes, grammar has to give way because the meaning is so clear."[33]

22

Names and Titles

Stand in someone else's shoes.[1]

—Justice Brett Kavanaugh

22.1 Guiding principle: Be consistent, impartial, and concise when naming individuals and using titles.

In a 2007 murder trial, the prosecutor used the defendant's nickname 29 times—and that choice led an appeals court to vacate the conviction. The reason? Defendant Laval Farmer, a member of the Bloods street gang, went by the nickname "Murder."[2]

Names have the power to characterize and to humanize. For good reason, Murder's defense counsel urged that his client be called "Mr. Farmer,"[3] using what's known as a courtesy title or honorific. Even "the Defendant" or his first or last name would be preferable to his prejudicial nickname.

In the same way, the justices choose names over generic references to tell individuals' stories. And by doing so, they show compassion and signal respect for the parties and to readers.

The Supreme Guide to Writing. Jill Barton, Oxford University Press. © Oxford University Press 2024.
DOI: 10.1093/oso/9780197754351.003.0022

22.2 Unanimous rule: Use consistent, unbiased names to tell a person's story but generic references to frame the bigger picture.

How writers name people can show bias and feed inequality. One study found it's twice as likely for writers to refer to male professionals using surnames, compared to female professionals, who are more likely to be identified by first name.[4] The study concluded, "this gender bias may contribute to the gender gap in perceived eminence as well as in actual recognition and may partially explain the persistent state of women's underrepresentation in high-status fields."[5]

The practice of using first names for women and surnames for men, to borrow from Justice Ginsburg's opinion in *United States v. Virginia*, "denies to women, simply because they are women, full citizenship stature—equal opportunity to aspire, achieve, participate in and contribute to society based on their individual talents and capacities."[6] Ginsburg further stated that "such classifications may not be used, as they once were, to create or perpetuate the legal, social, and economic inferiority of women."[7]

Likewise, the justices use consistent names (not varying classifications), for all individuals, to avoid showing gender bias when they describe the multiple players and parties in cases. They also recognize that the parties in lawsuits have names beyond *plaintiff, defendant, petitioner, respondent*, and so on. The justices use those names to describe the people behind the legal disputes, aiming to be concise and clear at every step.

In the next example, Justice Sotomayor uses the parties' names when relevant, with the full name on first reference and just the surname on later references. She opts for the concise *petitioners* only at points for ease of reading. Along with the vast majority of justices, she also skips the courtesy titles of *Mr.* and *Ms.* (That rule is detailed more in section 22.4.)

- **Larry Steven Wilkins** and **Jane Stanton** wanted quiet titles and
  a quiet road. **Wilkins** and **Stanton**, the **petitioners** here, both
  live alongside Robbins Gulch Road in rural Montana. The United
  States has permission, called an easement, for use of the road,
  which the Government interprets to include making the road
  available for public use. **Petitioners** allege that the road's public
  use has intruded upon their private lives, with strangers trespassing,
  stealing, and even shooting **Wilkins'** cat.[8]

Like the rest of the Court, Sotomayor doesn't complicate a party's
story by simultaneously referring to an individual by name and as
Claimant, *Plaintiff*, *Appellant*, and *Petitioner*. Though all references are
correct, mixing it up only confuses readers and forces them to make
sense of an often-complicated procedural history.

The justices use concise, consistent, and specific references to describe a party's plight and switch to generic names only when talking about the broader bearing of the case. For instance, here, Justice
Barrett uses a name while describing a party's specific argument but
generic terms when stating the broader rule.

- And while **Bartenwerfer** paints a picture of liability imposed
  willy-nilly on hapless bystanders, the law of fraud does not work
  that way. Ordinarily, a faultless **individual** is responsible for
  another's debt only when the two have a special relationship, and
  even then, defenses to liability are available. For instance, though
  an **employer** is generally accountable for the wrongdoing of
  an **employee**, he usually can escape liability if he proves that
  the **employee's** action was committed outside the scope of
  employment.[9]

In some cases, the aim of being consistent conflicts with the need
to be concise. In the next example, Barrett recounts a house sale
gone wrong and opts to take advantage of the rare need to use first
names only, referring to spouses as "Kate" and "David," to differentiate

between them. In this way, she avoids their clunky surname and streamlines the story.

- In 2005, **Kate Bartenwerfer** and her then-boyfriend, **David Bartenwerfer**, jointly purchased a house in San Francisco. Acting as business partners, the pair decided to remodel the house and sell it at a profit. **David** took charge of the project. . . .
Kate, on the other hand, was largely uninvolved. Like many home renovations, the **Bartenwerfers'** project was bumpier than anticipated. Still, they managed to get the house on the market, and **Kieran Buckley** bought it. . . . Yet after the house was his, **Buckley** discovered several defects that the **Bartenwerfers** had not divulged: a leaky roof, defective windows, a missing fire escape, and permit problems.[10]

But later, because the case focuses on the question of only Kate Bartenwerfer's liability, Barrett switches back to the unbiased surname for her, making clear in a parenthetical: "From now on, we will refer to Kate as 'Bartenwerfer.'"[11] She simplifies other terms as well:

- First, she is an "**individual debtor**." Second, the judgment is a "debt." And third, because the debt arises from the sale proceeds obtained by David's fraudulent misrepresentations, it is a debt "for money . . . obtained by . . . false pretenses, a false representation, or actual fraud." **Bartenwerfer** disputes the third premise.[12]

22.3 Unanimous rule: Use parentheticals to show shortened names only when needed to avoid confusion.

Some cases present an alphabet soup of names and parties. Barrett uses a single parenthetical in *Bartenwerfer* to keep various parties and players straight. That nod to simplicity is the rule in Court opinions.

The justices use parentheticals to show the shorthand for a name only when it's especially complicated—not as a matter of practice.

That means, if on the first reference Chief Justice Roberts writes a straightforward name, such as "Petitioner Jane Cummings," he doesn't follow it with the needless ("Cummings") or (Petitioner) (with or without quotation marks) to show he plans to shorten the name on subsequent references. Instead, on the second reference, Roberts simply writes "Cummings" because the reader knows exactly what he means:

- **Petitioner Jane Cummings** is deaf and legally blind, and communicates primarily in **American Sign Language (ASL)**. In October 2016, she sought physical therapy services from **respondent Premier Rehab Keller**, a small business in the Dallas-Fort Worth area. **Cummings** requested that **Premier Rehab** provide an **ASL** interpreter at her appointments.[13]

Roberts also doesn't explain that he's dropping "Keller" from the respondent's name, but he uses a parenthetical to make clear the lesser-known abbreviation for American Sign Language with "(ASL)."

Only a case with multiple players with more complicated names calls for a parenthetical indicating a shortened second reference. In this example, Barrett shows a shortened acronym for two government entities and a third parenthetical to indicate a collective reference.

- When an agency plans to undertake action that might "adversely affect" a protected species, the agency must consult with the U.S. Fish and Wildlife Service **(FWS)** and National Marine Fisheries Service **(NMFS) (together, "Services")** before proceeding.[14]

And here, Roberts shows an alternative avoiding the often-annoying parenthetical.

- In the summer of 2012, the Department of Homeland Security **(DHS)** announced an immigration program known as Deferred Action for Childhood Arrivals, **or DACA**.[15]

22.4 Majority rule: Skip gender-based courtesy titles: *Mr.*, *Ms.*, (and the forthcoming *Mx.*); but if you use one, avoid outdated and wordy references.

Perhaps nothing indicates the ever-increasing informality of legal writing more than the drop of gender-based courtesy titles in most Court opinions. While *The New York Times* stays true to tradition on this point, using *Mr.* and *Ms.* to name the personalities gracing its pages, the Court has largely abandoned the practice. The change belies other formalities at the Court, where every oral argument begins with a double honorific: "Mr. Chief Justice, and may it please the Court."

Only two justices have used the courtesy titles *Mr.* and *Ms.* to name the players in cases. (If you want to follow tradition and their lead, see section 22.5 for pointers.)

Given the old and new challenges presented by gender-based titles, it's no surprise that most justices have embraced informality here. In 2012, France banned the use of *Mademoiselle*, a title translating to *Miss*, in legal documents because it unnecessarily referred to a woman's young age or marital status. Feminist groups called for the change, arguing that "we don't call a single man 'mondamoiseau,' or even 'young male virgin'" and that "this sort of distinction is reserved for women."[16]

The decision followed similar bans in Germany, which no longer uses *Fraulein*, meaning "little woman," and Italy, where titles such as *Signorina* are not used in official documents.[17] A cultural shift in English-speaking countries also largely cancels out the use of *Miss* and *Mrs.* in favor of the more inclusive *Ms.*

The Court, over the last few decades, has adapted to that change,[18] avoiding *Miss* and *Mrs.* and the similarly outdated *Ma'am*, save for the rare historical reference. The following example is the sole reference to *Mrs.* in recent years—an exception because it refers to a 1918 letter from a woman who referred to herself that way:

- In writing to thank United States Senator John Walter Smith for his donation, committee treasurer **Mrs. Martin Redman** explained that "[t]he chief reason I feel as deeply in this matter [is that], my son, [Wm.] F. Redman, lost his life in France and because of that I feel that our memorial cross is, in a way, his grave stone."[19]

Nowadays, the justices keep it simple, using a person's full name on first reference and surname on second and subsequent references. Here, Roberts shows how to cut often-clunky courtesy titles.

- **Petitioners David and Amy Carson** reside in Glenburn, Maine. When this litigation commenced, the **Carsons'** daughter attended high school at Bangor Christian Schools (BCS), which was founded in 1970 as a ministry of Bangor Baptist Church. The **Carsons** sent their daughter to BCS because of the school's high academic standards and because the school's Christian worldview aligns with their sincerely held religious beliefs.[20]
- Petitioners **Chike Uzuegbunam** and **Joseph Bradford** want to challenge the constitutionality of speech restrictions at Georgia Gwinnett College. There are just a few problems: **Uzuegbunam** and **Bradford** are no longer students at the college.[21]
- Petitioner **Rose Mary Knick** owns 90 acres of land in Scott Township, Pennsylvania, a small community just north of Scranton. **Knick** lives in a single-family home on the property and uses the rest of the land as a grazing area for horses and other farm animals.[22]

The nearly unanimous practice to drop gender-based courtesy titles at the Court avoids the looming question of what to do about the gender-neutral *Mx.*[23] The Court hasn't yet published an opinion involving an individual who uses *Mx.*, a title for those who don't identify as being of a particular gender or don't want to be identified by gender.[24]

But the new-ish title has appeared in lower court opinions. Trial courts in California and Pennsylvania have used the title, with explanation: "The Court recognizes that Harmon is a non-binary individual who uses the gender-neutral title Mx. and the pronouns they/them."[25] But even in those cases, courts show their preference to skip titles, using *Mx.* only when required in a quote:

- The Amended Complaint alleges that on that occasion, Anderson "loudly began discussing **Mx. Doe's** gender dysphoria and testosterone treatment" despite **Doe** not being publicly "out" as gender nonbinary at the time.[26]

The guiding principle to drop gender-based titles also makes sense when writing to someone for the first time because writers shouldn't assume a recipient's gender from a name or photo. Instead, they should drop the *Ms.*, *Mr.*, and *Mx.* and use an individual's full name. For example, an email or letter could begin with the following:

- Good morning, Whitney Dutton,
- Dear Dana Somerstein:

22.5 Guiding Principle: If using gender-based courtesy titles, make certain of an individual's gender and use only on second and subsequent references.

Using *Mr.*, *Ms.*, or *Mx.* in writing is tricky. All are perhaps overly formal in today's less-formal world. Plus, *Mr.* and *Ms.* could wrongly assign gender to a person, and *Mx.* is appropriate only when an individual requests so explicitly.

Justice Gorsuch is the only justice still using gender-based courtesy titles,[27] and when he does, he gets two key things right: First, he uses the proper style, with an individual's full name on first reference and the title with the individual's surname on later references, as shown here:

- One evening in 2007, **Annette White** attended a gathering with **Ervine Davenport**. On the drive home, **Mr. Davenport** killed **Ms. White**. At trial, the only questions concerned why and how **Mr. Davenport** claimed self-defense and testified to that effect. On his account, **Ms. White** grew angry during the trip and tried to grab the steering wheel from him while he was driving.[28]

Second, Gorsuch makes clear that he's using the appropriate title. Here, he explains why he's using *Ms.* for Aimee Stephens, a plaintiff in the landmark case of *Bostock v. Clayton County, Georgia*, which held that employees cannot be fired for being gay or transgender.

- **Aimee Stephens** worked at R. G. & G. R. Harris Funeral Homes in Garden City, Michigan. When she got the job, **Ms. Stephens** presented as a male. But two years into her service with the company, she began treatment for despair and loneliness. Ultimately, clinicians diagnosed her with gender dysphoria and recommended that she begin living as a woman. In her sixth year with the company, **Ms. Stephens** wrote a letter to her employer explaining that she planned to "live and work full-time as a woman" after she returned from an upcoming vacation. The funeral home fired her before she left, telling her "this is not going to work out."[29]

Courtesy titles have a place in the legal profession, where showing deference keeps flat-out disagreements at a professional level. The justices use *Mr.* and *Ms.* each time they address an advocate in oral argument. Similarly, advocates use *Your Honor* and *Justice* in response, showing a need to master the style for professional titles as well.

22.6 Guiding principle: Be consistent and concise when using professional titles.

While most justices skip the generic titles of *Mr.* and *Ms.*, they bend to tradition with professional titles. They use *Chief Justice, Justice, Judge*, and so on when referring to their colleagues. They use *President, Governor, Secretary, Senator*, and the like to refer to elected officials, and *Officer, Deputy, Professor*, or *Doctor* to show respect toward law enforcement and other professionals.

But exactly how they use the titles varies between opinions. For well-known individuals, like presidents, they tend to use only the title and surname on each reference, except where confusion could arise. For others, they mostly use the professional title and full name on first reference, with the title and surname on later references.

Within each opinion, the justices are consistent in how they use professional titles—and opt for the concise over the clunky. There are exceptions. (Yes, yes, to nearly every rule. That's why we're here.) But the following examples explain how the justices typically use professional titles.

22.6.1 Guiding principle: For professional titles, use the title and full name on first reference and the title and surname on later references.

- The case's cast of characters are public officials who worked at or with the Port Authority and had political ties to **New Jersey's then-Governor Chris Christie**. . . . At the time relevant here, William Baroni was its Deputy Executive Director, an appointee of **Governor Christie** and the highest ranking New Jersey official in the agency.[30]
- According to his expert, **Dr. Joel Zivot**, while in this semiconscious "twilight stage" Mr. Bucklew would be unable to

prevent his tumors from obstructing his breathing, which would make him feel like he was suffocating. **Dr. Zivot** declined to say how long this twilight stage would last.[31]

- In the summer of 2007, then-**Professor Elizabeth Warren** called for the creation of a new, independent federal agency focused on regulating consumer financial products. **Professor Warren** believed the financial products marketed to ordinary American households—credit cards, student loans, mortgages, and the like—had grown increasingly unsafe due to a "regulatory jumble" that paid too much attention to banks and too little to consumers.[32]
- Two months later, Duke's successor, **Secretary Kirstjen M. Nielsen**, responded via memorandum. . . . **Secretary Nielsen** went on to articulate her "understanding" of Duke's memorandum, identifying three reasons why, in **Nielsen**'s estimation, "the decision to rescind the DACA policy was, and remains, sound."[33]

22.6.2 Guiding principle: For well-known individuals on all references, use the professional title and surname only.

- Congress passed and **President Ford** signed the Foreign Sovereign Immunities Act.[34]
- **President Eisenhower** signed the Compact.[35]

22.6.3 Guiding principle: When confusion could arise with well-known individuals, use the professional title and full name.

This might happen only with the five pairs of presidents and the few justices who share surnames, but history comes up in Supreme Court opinions. For Presidents named Adams, Bush, Harrison, Johnson, and Roosevelt, use the first name on first reference.

- After his election in 1904, **President Theodore Roosevelt**, who "shared the progressive faith in administrative expertise," sought to "rei[n] in judicial review" of administrative action.[36]
- Less than two years into Humphrey's term, newly inaugurated **President Franklin D. Roosevelt** wrote Humphrey a letter, asking for his resignation. . . . A little over a month after his first letter, **President Roosevelt** wrote Humphrey again to ask for his resignation.[37]
- In 2003, Congress passed and **President George W. Bush** signed the United States Leadership Against HIV/AIDS, Tuberculosis, and Malaria Act, known as the Leadership Act.[38]
- In 1991, Congress passed and **President George H. W. Bush** signed the Telephone Consumer Protection Act.[39]

22.6.4 Unanimous rule: Capitalize titles and names of government organizations.

The justices regularly reference what this President or that Governor did, or how a government agency acted. For brevity, they often use the capitalized title when referencing an individual or organization, whether it's specific or generic. They also capitalize Court when referring to the U.S. Supreme Court, distinguishing it from a district court or appellate court (which take lowercase letters). A few more examples:

- The **Commission** consists of two members, one appointed by the **Governor of New York** and the other by the **Governor of New Jersey**.[40]
- Indeed, **the Solicitor General** has informed the Court that the **President** supports such legislation as a matter of policy.[41]
- And if those principles do not apply or do not suffice to protect U.S. national security and foreign policy interests, **Congress** and the **President** may always respond by enacting additional legislation.[42]

- **The Secretary of Veterans Affairs** advances two reasons why
  §5110(b)(1) is not subject to equitable tolling. . . . We need not
  address the **Secretary's** first argument because the second is
  straightforward.[43]

22.6.5 Concluding guiding principle: For titles, be consistent.

While the justices remain consistent in their use of titles within each
opinion, their practices vary—so much so that pinpointing a majority
rule on this topic isn't doable. The next examples make plain the
many ways the justices use titles. For instance, the justices sometimes
drop a longer, formal title after the first reference to keep their syntax
concise, just as this book does for each chapter.

- **Chief Justice John Marshall**, who had recently squared off with
  the Jefferson administration in *Marbury v. Madison*, presided as
  Circuit Justice for Virginia. . . . Following four days of argument,
  Marshall announced his ruling to a packed chamber.[44]

Or sometimes, some justices use full names for well-known individuals.

- Five years after Hamilton wrote Federalist No. 78, **Secretary of
  State Thomas Jefferson** sent a letter on behalf of **President
  George Washington** to **Chief Justice John Jay** and the
  Associate Justices of the Supreme Court, asking for advice about
  the Nation's rights and obligations regarding the ongoing war in
  Europe.[45]

Other justices skip first names—on occasion. Justice Kavanaugh
skipped the first names for Presidents Obama and Trump,[46] while
Justice Thomas used *Barack* and *Donald* on his first references.[47] Here,
Thomas flip flops on his use of first names on first reference with the
title of *Senator*.

- **Senator Stephen Douglas**, defending Dred Scott a few months later in Springfield, Illinois, expressed the converse of Taney's reasoning.[48]
- For example, **Senators Sessions and Hatch** introduced legislation in 2001 to lower the ratio to 20 to 1.[49]

Here, Gorsuch uses no first name for Justice John Marshall Harlan, even though there were two. (The first served from 1877 to 1911, and his grandson served from 1955 to 1971.) But any confusion in this example is avoided by citing a 1969 Justice Harlan opinion.

- **Justice Harlan** called these divergent results "an extraordinary collection of rules."[50]

The point with these fluctuating examples is not to cause confusion, but instead to make plain that when it comes to titles, writers get it right with multiple formats. In general, the goal is to use names and titles in a way that's concise, consistent, and, above all, unbiased.

23

Negatives

What we can decide, we can undecide.[1]

—Justice Elena Kagan

23.1 Unanimous guiding principle: Use negative words sparingly and double negatives for precision.

One of Ernest Hemingway's four rules for writing was to pick positive language over negative. And mostly, the justices stick to this advice.[2] That means they typically opt for affirmative, shorter words like *late* instead of *untimely* or *not on time*.

But negative language is unavoidable in legal writing. Words such as *unreasonable, unlawful, unlicensed*, and *unpermitted* abound in constitutions and statutes. Laws, by nature, tend to prohibit, rather than permit, as shown with the triple negative in the Eighth Amendment: "Excessive bail shall *not* be required, *nor* excessive fines imposed, *nor* cruel and unusual punishments inflicted."

It's not impossible to find negatives and even double negatives in Supreme Court opinions—not the grammatically incorrect, but the legally complex kind. All the justices use negative wording and even double negatives on occasion to finesse a point, sometimes for emphasis, sometimes to cut out shades of gray. Among the most amusing: a line from Chief Justice Roberts: "That decision is as inexplicable as it is unexplained."[3] Here are a few more examples where the justices break the no-negative-wording rule.

The Supreme Guide to Writing. Jill Barton, Oxford University Press. © Oxford University Press 2024.
DOI: 10.1093/oso/9780197754351.003.0023

23.2 Unanimous rule: Use negative words sparingly, particularly when pairing *not* with words beginning in *in-* or *ir-* or *un-*.

Some writing experts will tell you to avoid the unnecessary flourish of phrases like "not insignificant"[4] or "not infrequently"[5] or "not un-lawful."[6] But all the justices occasionally draw out a point in this way.

- But they are **not inflexible** rules.[7]
- But reluctance is **not inability**.[8]
- Second there is **nothing irregular** about the history leading up to the September 2017 rescission.[9]
- That contention is **not without** some support.[10]
- This process is **not unlike** what legislatures do with statutes.[11]

Would the meaning be the same if Justice Thomas wrote, "This process is *like* what legislatures do"? Perhaps, but some nuance, and some flounce, would be lost.

Even so, most of the justices opt for this wordier option only once or twice a term. Overall, their use of positive wording far exceeds the negative. In five years, for instance, they used *reasonable* 926 times and *unreasonable* a mere 151 times, with many of those references in quotes. The takeaway: Keep the unnecessary negatives to a minimum and use them with purpose or the very occasional flourish.

23.3 Unanimous rule: Use double negatives when required for precision.

At times, the justices use a double negative to limit an interpretation. When Roberts writes, "the case is remanded for further proceedings *not inconsistent* with this opinion,"[12] the sentence implies the potential scope of the lower court's actions is narrower than if he wrote *consistent.* Consider how the meaning subtly shifts in these next examples when the negative wording is swapped for the positive.

- Respondents' argument **is not** that the Government exercised its statutory authority in an **unreasonable** fashion.[13]
  - Positive: Respondents' argument **is** that the Government exercised its statutory authority in a **reasonable** fashion.
- **Not** even the most crystalline abrogation can take effect **unless** it is "a valid exercise of constitutional authority."[14]
  - Positive: **Even** the most crystalline abrogation can take effect **if** it is "a valid exercise of constitutional authority."
- An offense **does not qualify** as a "violent felony" **unless** the least serious conduct it covers falls within the elements clause.[15]
  - Positive: An offense **qualifies** as a "violent felony" **if** the least serious conduct it covers falls within the elements clause.
- And **unless** an employer has a religious objection to the accommodation, it is **unclear** why an employer would give it up.[16]
  - Positive: And **when** an employer has a religious objection to the accommodation, it is **clear** why an employer would give it up.

24

Numbers

You've heard some of the numbers before.[1]

—Justice Elena Kagan

24.1 Unanimous guiding principle: Spell out numbers zero to nine or when starting a sentence.

Writing numbers can perplex the legal writer, and not just because few of us tend to be math whizzes. Previously, legal writing guides called for spelling out numbers below 50 or 100, and for using unnecessary parentheticals for a doublet, like *Plaintiff seeks $5 (five) million*. Not anymore, say the nine justices, who unanimously simplify the way they write numbers. They use simple numerals for measurements, money, time periods, dates, and numbers 10 and above. They spell out numbers zero to nine, generic references like *tens of billions*, and those starting sentences.

24.2 Majority rule: Write specific percentages with numerals and the percent symbol.

The only split among the justices on the question of numbers is whether to use the word *percent* or its corresponding symbol. A few of the justices are inconsistent on this point, but most use the symbol most of the time.

The Supreme Guide to Writing. Jill Barton, Oxford University Press. © Oxford University Press 2024.
DOI: 10.1093/oso/9780197754351.003.0024

- Before peremptory strikes even started, the venire had gone from **42%** to **28%** black.[2]
- The restriction on sales of **3.2%** beer to young men challenged by a drive-through convenience store in Craig was defended on "public health and safety grounds," including the premise that young men were particularly susceptible to driving while intoxicated.[3]

24.3 Unanimous rule: Use numerals for 10 and higher.

That means, spell out numbers zero to nine, along with fractions and generic numbers like *hundreds*.[4]

- Thus, all **five** courts are subject to the "bare majority" requirement, and **three** of the **five** courts are additionally subject to the "major party" requirement.[5]
- Over **three-quarters** of Alaska's **300** communities live in regions unconnected to the State's road system.[6]
- Over the last **33** years, **tens of thousands** of §924(c) cases have been prosecuted in the federal courts.[7]

But use numerals for 10 and above:

- At the very least, the defendant contended, any term of imprisonment should be less than **12** months long.[8]
- Before the City seized his car, Peake relied on his **200,000**-mile 2007 Lincoln MKZ to travel **45** miles each day from his home on the South Side of Chicago to his job in Joliet, Illinois.[9]

And measurements:

- Some States set residential cleanup levels as low as **0.04 ppm**.[10]
- The landowners also seek to capture and treat shallow groundwater through an **8,000-foot** long, **15-foot** deep, and

3-foot wide underground permeable barrier, a plan the agency rejected as costly and unnecessary to secure safe drinking water.[11]

And money and time periods and dates:

- The thief who loosens an already loose grasp or (assuming the angle is right) tears the side of a **$5** bill has hardly used any force at all.[12]
- So counting them makes the fraction smaller and reduces hospitals' payments considerably—by between **$3** and **$4** billion over a **9-year** period, according to the government.[13]
- Yet although he had been on death row since **1999**, and the State had set a date for his execution on November **6, 2018**, he waited until January **23, 2019**—just **15** days before the execution—to ask for clarification.[14]

24.4 Unanimous rule: Use numerals except when numbers are at the start (or near start) of a sentence.

As a matter of style, always spell out numbers at the start of a sentence.

- **Three** States have adopted *M'Naghten* plus the volitional test. **Ten** States recognize a defense based on moral incapacity alone. **Thirteen** States and the District of Columbia have adopted variants of the Model Penal Code test, which combines volitional incapacity with an expanded version of moral incapacity.[15]
- **Twelve** lanes with tollbooths feed onto the Bridge's upper level from the Fort Lee side.[16]
- Nearly **fifty** years ago, we held that a federal prosecutor could obtain information from a President despite assertions of executive privilege . . . .[17]
- **Two million** maps, in other words, is not many maps at all.[18]

24.5 General rule: Use numerals except when numbers need to be spelled out for consistency.

If a sentence has a mix of numbers above and below 10, and it would be jarring to use a mix of numerals and spelled-out-numbers, then spell them all out for consistency, as Justice Kagan does here:

- Borden's reckless assault conviction carried a sentence of **two** to **twelve** years; but had he been convicted of purposeful or knowing assault, the sentencing range would have been **three** to **fifteen** years.[19]

Just note that legal writers rarely face this problem, so use your judgment. Here, Kagan uses both formats. It works because *forty-eight* would be too clunky.

- By **one** count, across all subject matter areas, **48** agencies have heads (and below them **hundreds** more inferior officials) removable only for cause.[20]

25

Prepositions

Words are not pebbles in alien juxtaposition.[1]

—Judge Learned Hand

25.1 Unanimous guiding principles: Ignore the myth that prepositions can't end sentences, and cut out unnecessary ones for more concise writing.

The grammarians got it wrong, again. The justices unanimously reject the old adage that you can't end a sentence with a preposition. All nine make their writing more conversational by not forcing a fix to this archaic standard. They also keep their writing concise by cutting out the unnecessary prepositional phrase. Here's how they do it:

25.2 Unanimous rule: End a sentence with a preposition when the workaround is awkward or wordy.

The justices don't flout Boomer grammar rules just for fun. Pages upon pages of opinions have sentences without a preposition like *on*, *to*, or *with* hanging off the end. But the justices know that sometimes, a sentence is better when this old-timey preposition rule is broken, as Justice Gorsuch shows here:

The Supreme Guide to Writing. Jill Barton, Oxford University Press. © Oxford University Press 2024.
DOI: 10.1093/oso/9780197754351.003.0025

- Congress, of course, didn't list every public entity the statute would apply to.[2]

Reworking this sentence to avoid the preposition at the end would make it read: "Congress, of course, didn't list every public·entity *to which* the statute would apply." That doesn't flow like ordinary conversation (and it adds the extra *which*—something Chief Justice Roberts urges legal writers to avoid—see section 4.8). Here are a few more— just in case traditionalists need more proof:

- Thankfully, there is a clear path forward that avoids these concerns—the one we are already **on**.[3]
- And that is what the District Court in Maryland inquired **into**.[4]
- But if the parties' extended etymological debate persuades us of anything, it is that care is called **for**.[5]
- But the opinion does not say where that rule comes **from**.[6]
- That partly closed-door policy changes once a verdict is **in**.[7]
- But in so doing, Gundy ignores even the rest of the section that phrase is **in**.[8]

25.3 Unanimous rule: Cut out unnecessary prepositions to make sentences concise.

Prepositions can bog down legal writing. The worst offenders are phrases bookended by prepositions, like *by means of, in order to,* or *with regard to.* Writers should cut those altogether. Sometimes, the justices are stuck with using too many of these wordy phrases when quoting a poorly worded provision. This Nebraska statute at issue in *Pereida v. Wilkinson,* for example, uses a whopping nine prepositional phrases in just one sub-part:

- Under Nebraska law, a person commits criminal impersonation if he . . . (d) **Without** the authorization . . . **of** another and **with** the intent to deceive or harm another: (i) Obtains or records . . .

personal identifying information; and (ii) Accesses or attempts to access the financial resources **of** another **through** the use **of** . . . personal identifying information **for** the purpose **of** obtaining credit, money . . . or any other thing **of** value."[9]

You can tighten many prepositional phrases into shorter possessives, adjectives, adverbs, gerunds, and infinitives—and cut others altogether. Trimming seven of the nine prepositional phrases in the Nebraska statute cuts 19 words and eases its flow.

- Under Nebraska law, a person commits criminal impersonation if he. . . (d) **Without authorization** and **with the intent** to deceive or harm another: (i) Obtains or records . . . personal identifying information; and (ii) Accesses or attempts to access **another's financial resources using** personal identifying information **to obtain** credit, money . . . or another **valuable** thing.

Prepositions become problematic only when there are too many. Two or even three help glue together points but too many will dilute a sentence's worth. That's why Kagan writes:

- This suit arises **from** North Carolina's publication **of** some **of** Allen's videos and photos.[10]

And not this wordy rewrite:

- This suit arises **from** the publication **by** North Carolina **of** some **of** the video and photos **by** Allen.

Keep that tidiness in mind when pruning your own writing for unnecessary prepositions.

26

Pronouns

At the heart of liberty is the right to define one's own concept of existence, of meaning, of the universe, and of the mystery of human life.[1]

—Justices Sandra Day O'Connor, Anthony Kennedy, and David Souter

26.1 Guiding principle: Choose inclusive and clear pronouns.

After the protagonist falls for the title character in *The French Lieutenant's Woman*, he laments: "I say 'her,' but the pronoun is one of the most terrifying masks man has invented; what came to Charles was not a pronoun, but eyes, looks, the line of the hair over a temple, a nimble step, a sleeping face."[2]

Pronouns still terrify, and for new reasons. They are a form of shorthand that by their nature, too often fail to fully stand for what they're describing. Pronouns can create confusion when used improperly. What's more, gender pronouns can offend and exclude individuals who are non-binary or whose gender is undisclosed or unknown.

The justices have shown a willingness to use more inclusive pronouns. While some legal writing experts argue that the Court should go further and adopt the non-binary *they*,[3] the legal profession is not yet uniform in its approach. The rules below explain where things stand now, along with tips on fixing common pronoun mix-ups and making writing more inclusive.

The Supreme Guide to Writing. Jill Barton, Oxford University Press. © Oxford University Press 2024.
DOI: 10.1093/oso/9780197754351.003.0026

26.2 The 7–2 majority rule: Use inclusive pronouns.

At the first opportunity in 2020, a six-justice majority chose to use the correct personal pronouns when ruling in favor of a transgender woman.[4]

- **Aimee Stephens** worked at R. G. & G. R. Harris Funeral Homes in Garden City, Michigan. When **she** got the job, **Ms. Stephens** presented as a male. But two years into **her** service with the company, **she** began treatment for despair and loneliness. Ultimately, clinicians diagnosed **her** with gender dysphoria and recommended that **she** begin living as a woman.[5]

In a dissent, Justice Alito cautioned against potential impacts to free speech, arguing the "decision may even affect the way employers address their employees and the way teachers and school officials address students. . . . After today's decision, plaintiffs may claim that the failure to use their preferred pronoun violates one of the federal laws prohibiting sex discrimination."[6]

Likewise, the Harris Funeral Home's brief purposefully avoided using Stephens' correct pronouns, justifying, "Stephens's counsel indicates it is proper to refer to Stephens as 'she' and 'a woman.' Out of respect for Stephens and following this Court's lead in *Farmer v. Brennan*, Harris tries to avoid use of pronouns and sex-specific terms when referring to Stephens."[7]

Three years later, the Court's choice to use an individual's correct personal pronouns was confirmed in its ruling for a transgender immigrant. All 10 briefs filed in that case—on both sides—also used the correct pronouns.[8]

- Petitioner **Leon Santos-Zacaria** (who goes by the name Estrella) fled **her** native Guatemala in **her** early teens. **She** has testified that she left that country, and fears returning, because **she** suffered physical harm and faced death threats as a transgender woman who is attracted to men.[9]

In that case, Alito wrote a short concurrence on a jurisdictional question that did not reference Santos-Zacaria, so he used no personal pronouns.[10] Justice Thomas joined that concurrence, along with Alito's dissent in *Bostock v. Clayton County, Georgia*. It's unclear whether their silence in the 2023 case could signal acquiescence to the majority's use of inclusive pronouns, or a continuing objection. Thus, the majority rule to use inclusive pronouns settles at 7–2, awaiting another opportunity for Alito and Thomas to explicitly use what were once seen as non-traditional pronouns.

26.3 Unanimous rule: Avoid *he* as a universal pronoun.

On an easier pronoun question, the justices long ago abandoned the sexist use of the masculine *he* as the catchall pronoun. Eight justices rotate between *he* and *she* to be more inclusive, though some references stay true to stereotypical gender roles, such as casting a criminal or employer as a man and a victim as a woman.[11] But mostly, the justices swap in feminine pronouns for generic individuals routinely for inclusivity.

- Say a **customer** orders ceviche, a Peruvian specialty of raw fish marinated in citrus juice. Would **she** expect it to be cooked? No. Would **she** expect to pay full price for it? Again, no.[12]
- A **programmer** wishes, as part of **her** program, to determine which of two integers is the larger.[13]
- That kind of rule exists in federal court: There, an **expert witness** must produce all data **she** has considered in reaching **her** conclusions.[14]
- Suppose first that **a Maine citizen's** land is polluted by a nearby factory. **She** sues the company, alleging that it violated a federal environmental law and damaged **her** property.[15]

Additionally, when speaking hypothetically of a person, the justices at times opt to make their references plural, an easy way to avoid the need for a gender pronoun.

- **Companies** or **individuals** may be less likely to engage in intergovernmental efforts if **they** fear those activities will subject them to private suits.[16]
- First, it would be necessary for the **individuals** in question to believe that a religiously motivated party in the jurisdiction **they** left or avoided might engage in conduct that harmed **them**.[17]

Relatedly, six justices opt on occasion for the inclusive but wordy *he or she* phrase. Though the phrase is bemoaned as the "clunkiest phrase ever cooked up by small-minded grammarians,"[18] the justices use it in moderation—only 89 times in five years, largely in quotes or to refer to laws with the phrase. They also tend to offset the wordiness of the phrase with straightforward sentences, again proving the wordy option is the rare choice.

- Thus, unless the **customer** who borrowed $300 was aware of the fine print and actively prevented the loan's automatic renewal, **he or she** could end up having to pay $975, not $390.[19]
- To be sure, the **official** who makes the designation cannot delegate authority that **he or she** does not have.[20]
- Every **judge** must learn to live with the fact **he or she** will make some mistakes; it comes with the territory.[21]

26.4 Undecided through 2023: The non-binary *they*.

At the close of the 2022–23 term, the justices still had not confronted the question of whether to use the non-binary *they* as an individual's personal gender pronoun. But it's likely that question is coming. Given the Court's adoption of individuals' personal gender pronouns in *Bostock* and *Santos-Zacaria v. Garland*, it's likely the Court will use *they* for an individual using the pronoun.

In 2022, the U.S. Court of Appeals for the Seventh Circuit explained its use of the *they/their/them* for the appellant in a criminal case, citing the Supreme Court's use of *she* for Aimee Stephens in *Bostock* as support.

- Dyjak uses **they/them/their** pronouns in the briefs and motions in this case, and we have followed suit. We note in this connection that, despite the potential for some confusion about the singular and the plural, this usage of **"they/them/their"** has now been accepted by numerous style guides and dictionaries as appropriate in referring to a singular person of unknown or non-binary gender. We see no reason to break with that emerging consensus, in light of our normal practice of using the pronouns adopted by the person before us.[22]

26.5 Unanimous rule: Avoid the singular *they*.

Many writing experts advocate using the singular *they* to refer to non-binary individuals or those whose gender is unknown. In legal writing, the singular *they* also can describe individuals generically or those whose identity should be kept confidential, such as a minor, protected witness, or victim.[23] On this point though, the justices have stuck to tradition and unanimously avoided the singular, gender-neutral *they* in all published opinions (at least through 2023).[24]

That could change, given the Court's bent toward conversational language. Using a singular *they* is common in conversation, and a few justices drop it in oral argument.

- So why can't an employer tell **an employee** what **they're** permitted to do, personal or otherwise, during that time?[25]

- And even beyond that, I mean, I think actually, if you think about **the person** who wrote this language and why **they** wrote this language, it's—this language is written in recognition of the fact that there are sort of two—two sources of money that the IRS can try to collect from.[26]
- What if there's **nobody** who will do it for that reason, but **they** will do it if they get a little bit more money?[27]

But in writing, strict grammarians would say these sentences are incorrect, confusing the singular and the plural. And in writing, the Court has unanimously clung to that standard.

26.6 Unanimous rule: Use singular pronouns for singular collective nouns.

In the same way, the nine justices also agree that singular pronouns should represent collective nouns. A collective noun is a singular word referring to a group of people or things. Pronouns standing in for collective nouns should be singular. That means *it* should represent a court, parliament, commission, or company, despite those groups being made up of multiple individuals, as the Court shows here:

- Yamaha does not do the work the Court says **it** does.[28]
- But not always, as the **Court itself** recognizes.[29]
- Only in 1782 did **Parliament** finally relent, voting to expunge **its** prior resolutions and resolving that **its** actions had been "subversive of the rights of the whole body of electors of this kingdom."[30]
- When the **American Battle Monuments Commission** took over the project of designing the headstones, **it** responded to this public sentiment by opting to replace the wooden crosses and Stars of David with marble versions of those symbols.[31]

- As today's **plurality** rightly indicates in Part II–A, however,
  Lemon was a misadventure. **It** sought a "grand unified theory" of
  the Establishment Clause but left us only a mess.[32]
- To be fair, **Amgen** does not dispute this much. **It** freely admits
  that it seeks to claim for **itself** an entire universe of antibodies.[33]

Other common collective nouns that should be represented by *it*—or
its for the possessive and *itself* for the reflexive form—include *board*,
committee, corporation, family, jury, majority, appellate panel, or *staff*. Using
it for some collective nouns can seem awkward, as with *team*, where
many writers shift to using *they*.[34]

But the justices avoid this potential use of the singular *they* by
writing around the question, as good writers tend to do. For instance,
in a case centering on whether a high school football coach can pray
on the 50-yard line after games, the justices used *team* 44 times in the
majority opinion, concurrences, and dissent. But they never used a
pronoun for that word.[35] That shows why the unanimous rule for collective nouns is to stick with tradition.

Even so, the justices aren't always sticklers when speaking in oral
argument. Just as some justices use the gender-neutral *they* to represent a generic individual when speaking, they also opt for the plural
pronoun *they* for collective nouns at times in oral argument.

- And the **school district** says this goes too far, this is not the kind
  of mentor we want for our students. Can **they**—can the **District**
  do that?[36]
- I mean, **the state** doesn't have to provide collateral review of
  this particular claim, and **they're—they've** decided **they're** not
  going to.[37]
- Why shouldn't we wait for **Congress**? Now that the, you know,
  law has shifted, as Justice Alito pointed out, why isn't this the
  opportunity for **them** to act?[38]
- And . . . there's been some talk about, oh, it's **the IRS, they** just
  think that he owes money, but what is the process before the IRS
  decides he owes money?[39]

In writing, though, the justices always use singular pronouns for collective nouns, save for one sentence by Justice Alito, maybe chalked up to a mistake:

- And we opined that **Congress** would not have enacted the remaining minor provisions by **themselves**.[40]

While the choice to stick with singular pronouns for collective nouns follows traditional grammar rules, it doesn't necessarily follow tradition. In the Constitution, the founders repeatedly use *they* for the collective noun *Congress*. Conceivably, that's a nod to the democratic ideal that the word represents. Here, Chief Justice Roberts, writing for the majority, quotes one such clause:

- The Appointments Clause provides: "[The President] shall nominate, and by and with the Advice and Consent of the Senate, shall appoint Ambassadors, other public Ministers and Consuls, Judges of the supreme Court, and all other Officers of the United States, whose Appointments are not herein otherwise provided for, and which shall be established by Law: but **Congress** may by Law vest the Appointment of such inferior Officers, as **they** think proper, in the President alone, in the Courts of Law, or in the Heads of Departments."[41]

26.7 Unanimous rule: *Who* is for subjects; *whom* is for objects.

Unlike the previous pronoun questions, the answer to the *who* versus *whom* debate is certain, even if some writers find it elusive. Some speakers in casual conversation also might get it wrong purposefully, dropping the *m* in *whom* even when it's technically correct because *whom* can sound pompous.

The Supreme Court justices do not take that casual shortcut. Not when speaking in oral argument and not when writing opinions. In fact, they use the word in every minority opinion signed by more than one justice:

- JUSTICE THOMAS, with **whom** JUSTICE GORSUCH and JUSTICE BARRETT join, concurring in part and concurring in the judgment.[42]

Notably, the justices write *whom* rarely in comparison to *who*: 554 times versus 3,784 in five years. Many of those *whom* references either start minority opinions or come from quotes, which shows the justices likely write around the word at times, favoring plain language over pretension.

Pretension aside, some writers avoid *whom* because they're unsure whether *who* or *whom* is correct. Here's an easy trick to avoid any confusion. First, remember that *who* refers to subjects and *whom* refers to objects—in the same way that writers use *he* and *they* for subjects and *him* and *them* for objects. Now consider that writers don't typically confuse *he* with *him* or *they* with *them*, even though those pairs sound like *who* and *whom*, with all the pronouns for objects ending in *m*.

That mnemonic hint—*him*, *them*, and *whom* all end in *m*—can help writers figure out whether *who* or *whom* is correct. Here's how it works: When stuck on a *who* versus *whom* question, rewrite the sentences to use a different pronoun, as shown in these next examples. If *he* or *they* works, then *who* is correct. And if *him* or *them* is correct, then use *whom*. (Because *her*, also a correct pronoun for objects, doesn't have an *m*, put aside the need for that gendered pronoun for this trick.)

- At its head, Congress installed a single Director, **who/whom** the President could remove only "for cause."[43]
  ◦ the president could remove **him** → **whom**
- The FHFA is led by a single Director **who/whom** is appointed by the President with the advice and consent of the Senate.[44]
  ◦ **he** is appointed → **who**

- New Presidents always inherit thousands of Executive Branch officials **who/whom** they did not select.[45]
  - they did not select **them** → **whom**
- The chain of dependence between those **who/whom** govern and those **who/whom** endow them with power is broken.[46]
  - **he** governs and **he** endows → **who** and **who**

Another easy way to determine that *whom* is correct is when it's adjacent to a preposition, making it an object of the sentence, as with *about, for,* and *of* in the next sentences.

- Those cases safeguard particular choices **about whom** to marry; whom to have sex with; what family members to live with; how to raise children—and crucially, whether and when to have children.[47]
- And it would allow the statute, and the law, to work better and more simply **for those whom** it is meant to serve.[48]
- It employs over 400 seasonal workers and around 100 full-time workers, none **of whom** live on the property.[49]

26.8 Unanimous rule: Pronouns should not refer to ambiguous or nonexistent ideas.

"If this is starting to seem more confounding than clarifying, do not worry," promises Justice Gorsuch.[50] "This is not the stuff of which clear statements are made," explains Justice Jackson.[51] These statements could just as easily focus on pronouns as the jurisdictional questions they're actually addressing. Their imprecision casts doubt on the idea that indefinite pronouns, such as the blanket *it* and *this*, have no place in legal writing, where precision is key.

But a well-placed *it* or *this* can stand in for a complex set of ideas, arguments, or rules. These undefined pronouns help the legal writer summarize all that's important in just a few letters. All the justices use these not-perfectly-defined pronouns. The key is spelling out what the pronoun stands for in the preceding sentences or paragraphs.

With the Gorsuch and Jackson statements, the novice legal reader would have to take a close look at the opinions to figure out all that *this* stands for. It's there—it's just complicated. That's why a few letters summarizing a complex analysis aren't uncommon in Supreme Court opinions. Take this example, where Roberts devotes several paragraphs to explaining the plain meaning and background of a federal gaming law, along with a related Texas law and Tribal resolution. He then writes:

- So the breadth of the Tribe's request, and Congress's clear statement that it enacted § 107(a) in accordance with that request, strongly indicate that Congress intended to ban "all" gaming activities—"as defined by" Texas—that are inconsistent with Texas law. The Court does not view the Tribal Resolution as significant because Congress did not "purport to incorporate [it] into federal law." But **this** is not mere legislative history; it is statutory text.[52]

Syntacticians would argue that Roberts should have written more precisely, spelling out all that *this* entails, something like: *this background of the federal gaming law, Texas law, and Tribal resolution.* But even that doesn't capture all that Roberts had just explained. It would also be wordy and repetitive. It makes sense to use a pronoun shortcut, as the justices do at the end of every opinion, where they summarize what might have been a 50-page analysis with two letters: "**It** is so ordered."

The justices use this shortcut in other ways too, as a catchall and to underline an idea. The structure uses more words than necessary, but within the justices' arguments, that's the point. These sentence openers slow readers down, asking them to pay heed.

- **It** is important to understand, however, that, technically speaking, the majority is wrong.[53]
- **It** is far from clear what such a showing would entail, and the majority leaves the parties in the dark.[54]

- **It** is hard to imagine a clearer break from the past.[55]
- **It** is undisputed here that the edition is "devoted to Prince."[56]
- **It** is no more strange to say in this case that, regardless of whatever rights and duties the parties may have, the particular remedy of an FLRA order is unavailable.[57]

The takeaway is that pronouns representing big ideas do work, especially when used frugally. Problems arise when pronouns are non-existent or ambiguous enough to cause confusion. That can easily happen in complex fact patterns with multiple players, even when good writers know to clarify all pronouns in a story.

In the next paragraph, Justice Sotomayor conveys the facts involving Defendant Terence Tramaine Andrus, his four siblings, his mother, and her boyfriends. She uses pronouns for the first three, but only following a direct, same-sentence reference. That strategy helps readers easily match up each pronoun to its antecedent.

- There was also evidence that **Andrus himself** suffered physical abuse: **His mother** would beat **him** and **his siblings** with a board "until **she** got tired" and would enlist **boyfriends** to "hold the **children** down while **she** beat them" or beat **them** directly. Moreover, because **Andrus' mother** was so often absent or disoriented, **she** left **her children** to fend for **themselves** for extended periods, often without leaving **them** enough food to eat. Lacking a stable parental figure, **Andrus** assumed responsibility for **his** four **siblings** at around 12 years old: **He** would cook breakfast for **them**, get **them** ready for school, clean for **them**, help **them** with **their** homework, make **them** dinner, and put **them** to bed.[58]

In these three sentences, all 20 pronouns directly refer to their antecedent, allowing the story to cleanly unfold. A confusing mix of pronouns would distract from Sotomayor's argument and the story she wants running through her dissent. As she explains:

> "The art of persuasion is absolutely necessary to being both a good lawyer and a good judge. It's the same art that you need to tell a good

story. You have to persuade the person who's listening to you, whether in verbal speech or reading, that there's a purpose to what you're talking about, and you have to explain that purpose in a captivating way. . . . You have to have that power of storytelling."[59]

That power is possible only with rigorous editing. "Judges too must sometimes 'kill their darlings,'" Sotomayor said, referencing the oft-quoted advice from William Faulkner to cut those hard-won words. "Sometimes self-censorship is simply good craft and sensitivity to the purpose of one's words. If what I want a word to mean is not what others choose to understand by it, then I would do well to rephrase my argument, rather than claiming, like Humpty Dumpty to Alice, to be master of the word."[60]

With pronouns, becoming "master of the word" might seem like aiming for a trend-setting target. But Sotomayor's advice, to be sensitive "to the purpose of one's words," should prevail.

27

Qualifiers and Intensifiers

Like most rules, this one is not without exceptions or qualifications.[1]

—Chief Justice John Roberts

27.1 Unanimous rule: Use some qualifiers and intensifiers for conversational nuance.

If you strive to be a better writer, one challenge is that if you ask two great writers the same question, you might get opposite answers. Take qualifiers and intensifiers. Some writing experts argue to give them up.[2] But in fact, qualifiers and intensifiers can actually be quite useful and even somewhat fun—really.

Overdoing qualifiers and intensifiers, as that last sentence shows, can disrupt an otherwise fine point. But all the justices use qualifiers and intensifiers in moderation to maneuver through gray areas of the law or to add nuance to a rationale. Qualifiers, such as *quite* and *somewhat*, add vagueness to what would otherwise be a black-and-white description, while intensifiers, such as *really* and *very*, pile on to one's point. Here's a list of some of these less-than-specific descriptors:

Actually	Fairly	In fact	Just	Of course	Pretty	Quite
Rather	Really	So	Somewhat	Surely	That said	Very

Just, *rather*, and *so* are the most popular choices among the justices, while *pretty* and *that said* are used rarely and only by a minority of the justices. Keep in mind that much of the time legal writing demands precision. In this next sentence, Chief Justice Roberts doesn't write

The Supreme Guide to Writing. Jill Barton, Oxford University Press. © Oxford University Press 2024.
DOI: 10.1093/oso/9780197754351.003.0027

that the population of an endangered frog *rather* or *really* or *surely* dwindled; he gives specifics to paint a picture:

- By 2001, the known wild population of the dusky gopher frog had dwindled to a group of 100 at a single pond in southern Mississippi.[3]

The key here, as is often the case, is to use modifiers on occasion to add nuance and a conversational tone. Even the most informal of the nine—Justice Gorsuch—doesn't overdo it. In nearly 1,500 pages over five years, he used his two favorites, *just* and *really*, about 500 times total—so about once every three pages. And his opinions are the livelier for it.

- Is the majority **just** stretching to claim some cover for its novel arguments? Or does it **actually** mean to adopt the theory it professes to adopt?[4]
- If Congress **really** had wanted all exemptions to cease after a temporary period, that was **surely** an odd way to achieve it.[5]
- It is thus unsurprising—and **in fact quite** helpful for later review—that the IJ addressed many of those questions at length.[6]
- That's a **pretty** good clue something has gone wrong.[7]
- And, **of course**, federal courts possess no authority to issue rulings beyond the cases and controversies before them.[8]
- The majority's conclusion that a single use of the word "seizures" bears two different meanings at the same time—indeed, in this **very** case—is **truly** novel.[9]
- Ultimately, it's hard not to wonder whether the majority says **so** little about the Constitution's terms because **so** little can be said that might support its ruling.[10]

So the justices don't shy away from tempering their points with qualifiers or augmenting them with intensifiers. Even the loathsome *literally*, what writing guru Benjamin Dreyer called the "respectable word that has been distorted into the Intensifier from hell,"[11] appears 43 times (outside of quotes) in five years. In some cases, the justices even double up. But at least they use *literally* correctly (unlike Dreyer's cautionary example: "No, you did not literally die laughing.").[12]

- Now, under this Court's order, tens of thousands of absentee voters, unlikely to receive their ballots in time to cast them, will be left **quite literally** without a vote.[13]
- During what has been called the "high plenary power era of U.S. Indian law," this Court sometimes took the word "plenary" **pretty literally**.[14]
- Examples abound. An "American flag" could **literally** encompass a flag made in America, but in common parlance it denotes the Stars and Stripes. A "three-pointer" could **literally** include a field goal in football, but in common parlance, it is a shot from behind the arc in basketball. A "cold war" could **literally** mean any wintertime war, but in common parlance it signifies a conflict short of open warfare. A "washing machine" could **literally** refer to any machine used for washing any item, but in everyday speech it means a machine for washing clothes.[15]
- Read **literally**, the statute would cover a surgeon accessing a vein of a person in the street.[16]

28

Relative Pronouns

When, Where, Who, Whom, and Whose

This depends upon the meaning of the relative pronoun "which."[1]

—Justice Benjamin Curtis

28.1 Unanimous rule: Use commas around only essential clauses.

Too many commas litter legal writing. The comma debate with *that* and *which* is an easy one to solve (and covered in section 4.8). But other relative pronouns—*when, where, who, whom,* and *whose*—pose a trickier question. Quick refresher: Always skip the commas for clauses beginning with *that* because they're essential to a sentence. But always add commas for clauses beginning with *which,* because as a matter of grammar, they can be cut from a sentence.

The trick to figuring out whether clauses beginning with *when, where, who, whom,* and *whose* need commas is figuring out whether they're essential or not. That is, if you cut the clause, would the sentence still work? If yes, then it needs commas to offset the non-essential detail. If no, then the clause is essential, so skip the commas.

The next pairs of examples illustrate the difference. The clauses in the first sentences have no commas because they add essential information. The clauses in the second sentences have commas around non-essential information. In other words, when clauses add detail that's not essential to a sentence's basic meaning, commas should offset those clauses.

The Supreme Guide to Writing. Jill Barton, Oxford University Press. © Oxford University Press 2024.
DOI: 10.1093/oso/9780197754351.003.0028

- We have repeatedly held that the Establishment Clause is not offended **when** religious observers and organizations benefit from neutral government programs.[2]
- By the summer of 1787, **when** the delegates met in Philadelphia, state interference with interstate commerce was cutting off the lifeblood of the Nation.[3]
- The memory loss is genuine: Let us say the person has some kind of amnesia, which has produced a black hole **where** that recollection should be.[4]
- He then went to trial, **where** he was not permitted to advance a treaty-based defense, and a jury convicted him on both counts.[5]
- Consider initially a person **who** cannot remember his crime because of a mental disorder, but who otherwise has full cognitive function.[6]
- Residents of those areas include many of Alaska's poorest citizens, **who** rely on rivers for access to necessities like food and fuel.[7]

For tips on when to use *who* versus *whom*, see section 26.7.

- The steps were straightforward: Albo would ask Van Buren to search the state law enforcement computer database for a license plate purportedly belonging to a woman **whom** Albo had met at a local strip club.[8]
- (Alexander Hamilton secured his place on the Broadway stage— but possibly in the cemetery too—by lobbying Federalists in the House to tip the election to Jefferson, **whom** he loathed but viewed as less of an existential threat to the Republic.)[9]
- When the vote comes in, Washington moves toward appointing the electors chosen by the party **whose** candidate won the statewide count.[10]
- So too, John Jay predicted that the Electoral College would "be composed of the most enlightened and respectable citizens," **whose** choices would reflect "discretion and discernment."[11]

29

Short Words—and Sentences

If Congress had wanted the provision to have that effect, it could have
said so in words far simpler than those that it wrote.[1]

—Chief Justice John Roberts

29.1 Unanimous rule: Keep it short.

In Shakespeare's time, the average sentence ran nearly 50 words.[2] So
it's curious that the era's most famous writer is known for his short
quips: "To be or not to be." "All that glitters is not gold." And: "A
horse, a horse! My kingdom for a horse!"[3]

The same thinking guides the justices' writing. While they drop
some Faulkner-esque sentences in their opinions, most are short—
averaging around 18 words.[4] What's more, the vast majority of their
words are short, not unlike Shakespeare's, averaging six letters or
fewer.[5]

Justice Kagan's clever opening in a dissent about a confession typifies
that casual tone. The sentences here average just 15 words. Her words
average a mere five letters. With each line, Kagan speeds the reader
along, showing that good legal writing is simple but not simplistic.

- Imagine a criminal case involving two defendants—John and
  Mary. John and Mary are arrested for robbing Bill. Before trial,
  John confesses to the robbery in an interview with police. But
  John does more than admit his own involvement; he also points
  a finger at Mary. John says to the police: "Mary and I went
  out Saturday night and robbed Bill." Mary, on the other hand,
  never confesses to the robbery. She maintains that she wasn't

The Supreme Guide to Writing. Jill Barton, Oxford University Press. © Oxford University Press 2024.
DOI: 10.1093/oso/9780197754351.003.0029

involved—in fact, that she never left her home on the night in question. The government tries John and Mary together. At trial, it introduces a copy of John's confession into evidence, and has it read to the jury by the interviewing officer. But John elects not to take the stand, leaving Mary's attorney without an opportunity to cross-examine him about his confession.[6]

Kagan says her seemingly effortless, conversational style "takes a ton of work" and time: "Mostly I think writing is really hard," she told Harvard Law School students in 2017:.

> "I do a lot of drafts. I stare at the same paragraph for hours at a time. I can stare at the same sentence for hours at a time. It takes work. It takes time. And you have to be willing to devote it, to in the end, get a final product that looks as though it's all just flowed from your pen."[7]

Skim any opinion, and there's no shortage of short sentences shaped by short words. Judges have been known to use seemingly made-up words now and again. (Justice Scalia not only employed "jiggery-pokery," but also "argle-bargle"[8] and "tutti-frutti."[9]) But the justices typically opt for a simple, punchy word, over a complex counterpart.

The justices take pains not just to prune longer words and sentences from their opinions but also to add variety. Chief Justice Roberts shows just that with this gem: "Bust followed boom."[10] To further illustrate, here are a few of the pithier lines from each of the six authors in a landmark 2023 affirmative action case.[11]

- Chief Justice Roberts: So too in other areas of life. . . . Universities may define their missions as they see fit. The Constitution defines ours.[12]
- Justice Thomas: The stakes are simply too high to gamble.[13]
- Justice Sotomayor: No one is fooled.[14]
- Justice Gorsuch: There are clear losers too.[15]
- Justice Kavanaugh: The dissents suggest that the answer is yes. But this Court's precedents make clear that the answer is no.[16]
- Justice Jackson: History speaks. In some form, it can be heard forever.[17]

30

Split Infinitives

> But relying on this grammatical sleight of hand does not exactly help
> the Commissioner's argument that the text is clear.[1]
>
> —Justice Amy Coney Barrett

30.1 Unanimous rule: Split up those infinitives—and other verb phrases too.

To boldly split or not to split? Grammarians debate and often discourage splitting infinitives, or breaking up a verb phrase with a modifying word or phrase.[2] The iconic Star Trek line, "to boldly go where no one has gone before," breaks up the verb phrase *to go* with *boldly*.

All nine justices are bold here too, shirking grammarians' timeworn advice. The old rule stems from the fact that the infinitive is just one word in Latin, so it can't be split.[3] But in English, the infinitive is two words, as in *to hold* or *to offer*. The justices recognize that a truth about Latin can't extend to our legal writing today. All break up infinitives with adverbs.

Many times, splitting the infinitive just sounds better, as Justice Kagan shows here:

- Second, a person suffering from dementia may be unable **to rationally understand** the reasons for his sentence; if so, the Eighth Amendment does not allow his execution.[4]
- Those mechanisms did not (as the term rule did) aid the trial court to get its decision right in the first instance; rather, they served **to collaterally attack** its already completed judgment.[5]

The Supreme Guide to Writing. Jill Barton, Oxford University Press. © Oxford University Press 2024.
DOI: 10.1093/oso/9780197754351.003.0030

In some cases, not splitting the infinitive would confuse the meaning. In the next example, consider that if Justice Thomas moved the word *quickly* in the longer verb phrase, the meaning would shift.

- A programmer familiar with prewritten methods can string many of them together **to quickly develop** complicated programs without having to write from scratch all the basic subprograms.[6]

Thomas didn't want to write *can string many of them together quickly* or *to develop quickly complicated programs*. So he split the infinitive to keep *quickly* close to exactly what it modified: *develop*.

Even so, the justices opt for strong verbs (see Chapter 32). That means they often skip adverbs (see Chapter 17)—what some consider a crutch that weakens writing. And just because they reject the no-splitting-infinitives-myth doesn't mean they don't keep infinitives together when it best serves the sentence. Justice Ginsburg, along with a few other justices, never broke up her infinitives. That works, too (though it sounds less conversational).

- Defendants, after all, have good reason **promptly to raise** an objection that may rid them of the lawsuit filed against them. A Title VII complainant would be foolhardy **consciously to take** the risk that the employer would forgo a potentially dispositive defense.[7]

30.2 Additional rule: Split up longer verb phrases too.

Some grammar teachers have nonsensically extended the non-rule for infinitives to other verb phrases as well. Consider the modifier rule here (see Chapter 21): When using an adverb, keep it close to the verb it modifies. Sticking adverbs at the beginning or end of a longer verb phrase could muddle the meaning.

- Yet documents discussing such dead-end ideas **can hardly be described** as reflecting the agency's chosen course.[8]
- And in their appeal of the dismissal, they would be free **to also seek** review of the order denying class certification.[9]
- The Court, in turn, **strives mightily to refute** Gamble's account of the common law.[10]

31

Transitions

[T]he parties changed positions as nimbly as if dancing a quadrille.[1]

—Justice Robert H. Jackson

31.1 Unanimous rule: Ease the reader's way with transitions.

When Justice Sotomayor lambasted a majority opinion allowing life sentences for children, she did so point by point with explicit shifts: *First, second, third, next, thus, otherwise,* and *finally.* Her rebuke was methodical, each part carefully crafted to propel readers to the next, stacking the supporting law on top of itself along with emotional pleas, including this quote from the defendant: "please give me just one chance to show the world, man, like, I can be somebody."[2]

In legal writing, where the connection between A and B can have such weighty implications, transitions don't just avoid choppy writing. They seamlessly link facts to precedent, ideas to arguments, and rationales to conclusions. These shifts help show the reader exactly how each statement helps shape our system of laws.

All the justices use a variety of transitions to tie together what can amount to dozens of points in a 50-page opinion. The common features: each transition has meaning, orients readers, and impels readers forward.

Transitions often signal that there's an additional point on the same issue, as Sotomayor does in her dissent with *first, second, third,* and so forth. The everyday transitions including *and, also, on top of all that,* and *what's more* work great here. They're also far more common than their

The Supreme Guide to Writing. Jill Barton, Oxford University Press. © Oxford University Press 2024.
DOI: 10.1093/oso/9780197754351.003.0031

longer counterparts: *additionally, further, furthermore, furthermore, in addition*, and *moreover*. Full statements work too:

- The second move has issues too.[3]
- That observation points the way to another.[4]
- There is still more.[5]

Other purposes for transitions are introducing, comparing, contrasting, preempting, emphasizing, showing time or place, and concluding. These next examples show how the justices transition between points with these various purposes—with a single word, a phrase, or statement.

Introductory transitions announce a starting place or a new topic.

- **To begin with**, experience shows that Bielski is incorrect.[6]
- **For one thing**, the record is much less uncertain than the Government acknowledges.[7]
- **Start at square 1**, with what a trademark is and does.[8]
- **We begin** with the text.[9]

Comparison transitions describe similarities between ideas and include *equally, likewise, similarly, whereas*. Piling them up, as in the next example, piles up the support for a point. Among the most popular transition sentences—used by all nine—is *so too here*. The Court first used this phrase in 1865, and it appeared 28 times in the last five terms. Chief Justice Roberts gets extra credit (and shows the phrase's longevity) for dropping it into a 2003 brief.[10]

- **Like the statutes** at issue in these cases, the statute here contains a scienter provision. Section 841 states: "Except as authorized by this subchapter, it shall be unlawful for any person *knowingly or intentionally* . . . to manufacture, distribute, or dispense . . . a controlled substance." (Emphasis added.) **Like those three cases**, the question here concerns the mental state that applies to a statutory clause ("[e]xcept as authorized") that does not immediately follow the scienter provision. **Like the three cases,** the statutory clause in question plays a critical role in separating a defendant's wrongful from innocent conduct. And, **like the Court** in those cases, we conclude that the statute's mens rea applies to that critical clause.[11]

- **Just as it did for aggravated felonies**, Congress included "obstruction of justice" in the list.[12]
- **For similar reasons**, the Government's argument about legislative acquiescence is unavailing.[13]
- Can a potential hijacker use pâté jars **in the same way** as soda cans?[14]
- **Much like** Texas today, California in 1987 permitted bingo in various circumstances (including for charitable purposes), but treated deviations from its rules as criminal violations.[15]
- **Just as there is** no such duty with respect to the land, **there likewise is** no such duty with respect to the water.[16]
- Umpires in games at Wrigley Field do not defer to the Cubs manager's in-game interpretation of Wrigley's ground rules. **So too here**.[17]

Contrasting transitions introduce a competing thought. The best of these (and by far the most common) are the shortest: *but*, *still*, and *yet*. Other words that work here: *conversely*, *despite*, *however*, *nevertheless*, *nonetheless*, *notwithstanding*, *rather*, and *unlike*.

- **Nor** is this the only incongruity the government's theory invites.[18]
- Mary, **on the other hand**, never confesses to the robbery.[19]
- **In contrast**, the principal dissent cannot decide whether it favors such a categorical rule.[20]
- **Not so.** The *expressio unius* canon is a general rule, inapplicable where context suggests otherwise—as it does here.[21]
- Today, §1331 provides that "district courts shall have original jurisdiction of all civil actions arising under the Constitution, laws, or treaties of the United States." **Not** *may* have jurisdiction, **but** *shall*. **Not** *some* civil actions arising under federal law, **but**

all. The statute is as clear as statutes get, and everyone agrees it encompasses the claims Ms. Cochran and Axon seek to pursue. End of case, right? **Not so fast**.[22]

- **Think of it another way**.[23]

Preempting transitions can qualify or moderate, announcing the writer will head off a counterargument, refute a party's position, or perhaps, issue a stinging rebuke. These include *although, though, even though, at any rate, at least, in spite of, still*, and *even if*.

- **Granted**, the district court might backtrack, but if the question is purely legal, that is because of law books, not trial exhibits.[24]
- **While it may be true, in some sense**, that Smagin has felt his economic injury in Russia, focusing solely on that fact would miss central features of the alleged injury.[25]
- **Of course**, usually does not mean always.[26]
- **But even assuming that is true**, it does not mean that these laws were historical aberrations.[27]

Emphasizing transitions call attention to what's to come, often showing that the writer will illustrate or expand on a point. *For example, in fact, specifically*, and *to be sure* are standard. The justices also use *crucially, especially, in particular, namely, to explain, to illustrate*, and these:

- **Say** a getaway driver sees a pedestrian in his path but plows ahead anyway, knowing the car will run him over.[28]
- **For instance**, a green truck and a green hat are relevantly similar if one's metric is "things that are green."[29]
- **All the more so here**, where the State achieves its unconstitutional aim using novel procedural machinations that the Court fails to acknowledge.[30]
- **Without a doubt**, 2 Live Crew transformed Orbison's song by adding new lyrics and musical elements, such that "Pretty Woman" had a new message and different aesthetic than "Oh, Pretty

Woman." **Indeed**, the whole genre of music changed from rock ballad to rap.[31]

- There would be a number of issues to work through if *Smith* were overruled. **To name a few**: Should entities like Catholic Social Services—which is an arm of the Catholic Church—be treated differently than individuals?[32]

Temporal and spatial transitions orient the reader to a place or a moment in time. While plenty of sentences begin with straightforward clauses such as "In the 19th century," or "On the other side,"[33] the justices spice up their writing with variations.

- **From start to finish and over the course of nearly 100 pages**, they defend the universities' purposeful discrimination between applicants based on race.[34]
- **It was not until half a century later**, in *Brown*, that the Court honored the guarantee of equality in the Equal Protection Clause and Justice Harlan's vision of a Constitution that "neither knows nor tolerates classes among citizens."[35]
- **Fast forward now to a cold November morning in 2014**, when Wooden responded to a police officer's knock on his door.[36]
- **Since the first days of British rule**, the Crown oversaw—and retained the power to dictate—the Colonies' engagement with the Indian Tribes.[37]
- **Fast forward to the present**.[38]

Conclusory transitions explain a cause-and-effect or show the writer is wrapping up. *For these reasons, all in all, so*, and *thus* are among the most frequent in opinions' closing lines. Other transitions that draw things to a close include *all in all, as a result, at bottom, at its core, hence, in any event, in short, in sum*, and *in the end*. Here are a few more:

- **And so to recap**, focusing on the matter we suggested you attend to.[39]

- **Up to the last step**, the theory is unexceptionable—except that it points to MOHELA as the proper plaintiff.[40]
- **From the first page to the last**, today's opinion departs from the demands of judicial restraint.[41]
- **That is why** the law does not require Steven Spielberg or Banksy to make films or art for anyone who asks.[42]
- **In the end**, the Court cannot fault our predecessors for today's decision.[43]
- A mentally ill defendant may argue there that he is not blameworthy **because** he could not tell the difference between right and wrong. **Or, because** he did not know his conduct broke the law. **Or, because** he could not control his behavior. **Or, because** of anything else.[44]
- **Now consider one last option**.[45]
- **And there's the rub**.[46]

32

Verbs

Note the tense: "was," not "is."[1]

—Justice Elena Kagan

32.1 Unanimous guiding principle: Choose strong, active verbs.

The justices don't just *confront* or *deal* with legal issues. They *grapple, battle, tangle, tackle, unravel, delve, combat, ferret out, fumble,* and *plow* through them. They pick powerful verbs to expound on the scenes playing out in cases. They take care to elect exactly the right action, choosing everyday verbs along with more singular ones.

The basic lessons here: keep subjects and verbs close, and make sure the subject and verb match, especially in complicated sentences. The more advanced lessons: Pick a variety of dynamic, active verbs over inert, passive ones or nominalizations, which are verbs disguised as clunky nouns and adjectives. Use vigorous verbs to energize your writing or create a flowing cadence. Or skip the verb altogether (see Chapter 12 on fragments).

32.2 Unanimous rule: Keep subjects and verbs close together.

The term *legalese* exists because lawyers and lawmakers cram too many convoluted terms and clauses into too many sentences. It confuses, in part, because complex sentences often push the main subject and verb

The Supreme Guide to Writing. Jill Barton, Oxford University Press. © Oxford University Press 2024.
DOI: 10.1093/oso/9780197754351.003.0032

so far apart that the meaning is hard to find. Take this whopping, 191-word selection from the Federal Disposition Act.

> "Where any sum is payable on a money order, traveler's check, or other similar written instrument (other than a third party bank check) on which a banking or financial organization or a business association is directly liable—if the books and records of such banking or financial organizations or business association show the State in which such money order, traveler's check, or similar written instrument was purchased and the laws of the State of purchase do not provide for the escheat or custodial taking of the sum payable on such instrument, **the State** in which the banking or financial organization or business association has its principal place of business **shall be entitled to escheat or take custody** of the sum payable on such money order, traveler's check, or similar written instrument, to the extent of that State's power under its own laws to escheat or take custody of such sum, subject to the right of the State of purchase to recover such sum from the State of principal place of business if and when the law of the State of purchase makes provision for escheat or custodial taking of such sum."[2]

As with many statutes, this law pays no heed to the government's own advice to use plain language. It separates the subject and verb by a few lines and borders both with thorny clauses. "The natural word order of an English sentence is subject-verb-object," advises the Plain Language government working group, a collaboration of federal employees from different agencies who promote the use of clear communication in government writing. "This is how you first learned to write sentences, and it's still the best way."[3]

The justices know the best way. They can't sidestep legal terms like *escheatment*, but when the need to use one arises, they purposefully avoid twisting too many words around legal jargon. Justice Jackson's first opinion dissected that labyrinthine wording of the Federal Disposition Act, in a dispute among states over money orders. She began with the obligatory legal term but paired it with the simplest verb, *is*, and kept the subject exactly next to the verb.

- **"Escheatment" is** the power of a State, as a sovereign, to take custody of property deemed abandoned.[4]

Keeping subjects and verbs close is the best way to keep writing concise and clear. Every good writer varies sentence length, fluctuating between simple, punchy statements and compound sentences, some with multiple clauses. The next examples show how the justices achieve the former, with some dynamic verb choices—all placed exactly next to their subjects.

- And **that test knocked out** Jack Daniel's claim, whatever the likelihood of confusion.[5]
- Today, **the Court guts** *Miller v. Alabama* and *Montgomery v. Louisiana.*[6]
- By the 1950s, **Alaskans hankered** for both statehood and land—and **Congress decided** to give them both.[7]
- **The 1934 Act sweeps** more broadly.[8]
- **That determination flouts** over a century of this Court's practice.[9]

These crisp sentences leave no room for misunderstanding. They don't just keep the subjects and verbs close, but they also place adverbs, prepositional phrases, and objects adjacent to their matching verbs. This structure creates a more readable and forceful sentence.

32.3 Unanimous rule: Make sure subjects and verbs match, especially in complex sentences.

Keeping the subject and verb close also lessens the chance for mismatches between the subject and verb. Consider the next sentences, in which the singular subjects require singular verbs (as they always do). But intervening clauses put a plural word (*plaintiffs*, *technicians*, and *practices*) right next to the singular verb.

This arrangement can cause newer or hurried writers to misstep, particularly when sentences become longer and more complicated. While it's not wrong to write elongated sentences, it's always wrong to pair a single subject with a plural verb, or the other way around. In these next sentences, the justices make it complicated, but they get it right.

- The Court's related and highly functionalist **argument** that petitioners must be subject to the FLRA because they "exercise the authority of" an agency in supervising the **technicians** similarly **fails**.[10]
- Congress's **directive** to "continu[e]" existing administrative **practices does not evince** approval of any particular practice or prevent a court from saying that a particular practice has been unlawful all along.[11]
- A single administrative **decision**, like a single or even "a smattering of lower court **opinions**," **is** ordinarily not especially probative of statutory meaning.[12]

Readers can lose their place, or their focus, when a sentence's subject and verb fall lines apart on the page. The law requires complicated explanations, and sometimes, that calls for complicated sentences. But that doesn't mean the simplest sentences can't get the job done. The best practice is to avoid awkward, wordy constructions and keep the subject and verb close.

32.4 Unanimous rule: Prefer active to passive voice, except to change a sentence's emphasis.

"History speaks," Jackson wrote, dissenting in her first term.[13] For good reason, she didn't write, *The speaking is being done by history*. That passive voice construction isn't wrong, grammatically speaking. But it's verbose and lifeless, as passive voice tends to be. That's why good writers typically avoid it.

Passive voice puts the action in the background because it emphasizes what's being acted upon, or the object of a sentence. The

construction is convenient when writers don't know who is performing an action or want to leave the person or subject out of a
sentence. It's a good trick when a politician needs to admit, *mistakes
were made.*[14]

Swapping that statement to active voice uses the same number of
words: *I made mistakes.* But the sentiment is decidedly different. Passive
voice keeps the politician out of the spotlight, even though everyone
knows it's the politician who made the mistakes.

Passive voice played a starring role in one 2023 case, but not in a
good way. The case starts with Kate Bartenwerfer filing for bankruptcy. Bankruptcy law forgives some debts so people can get a "fresh
start," but not if the person is in debt because of fraud.[15] That exception in the law uses passive voice, prohibiting the forgiveness of debts
"obtained by . . . fraud."

Just like the politician's statement, *mistakes were made*, doesn't specify who made the mistakes, the bankruptcy law's statement, *obtained
by fraud*, doesn't specify who committed the fraud. And Bartenwerfer
didn't commit the fraud. Her husband did. A lower court said she was
liable for his debts, and she wanted bankruptcy to forgive those debts.

Bartenwerfer tried to use the passive voice in the provision to her
advantage. If everyone understands the politician committed the mistakes because it's implied, then it's also implied that only the person
who committed the fraud can't have his debts forgiven. More specifically, Bartenwerfer argued: "An ordinary English speaker would
understand that 'money obtained by fraud' means money obtained by
the *individual debtor's* fraud."[16]

But that interpretation adds something to the law that isn't there,
Justice Barrett wrote for a unanimous Court. The whole point of
passive voice is that it "pulls the actor off the stage."[17] It leaves the
politician out of the sentence about mistakes, and it leaves the specific
fraudster out of the bankruptcy law.

Though it's ambiguous by nature, all the justices use passive voice
at times. Like all good writers, they favor active voice because it's

more direct and concise. When they use passive voice, it's purposeful, altering a sentence's emphasis or deflecting attention from the actor.

Passive voice is wordier because its verb form requires two or more words, while a direct verb can be just the one. Passive voice can make sentences even more rambling if the writer wants to identify who or what is doing the action—because passive voice relegates that actor to a prepositional phrase. Justice Kagan shows both versions of passive voice here:

- His work **has been copied** so often that *Rolling Stone* (whose name **was partly inspired by—OK, you guessed it—Bob Dylan**) recently published a list of the 80 greatest Dylan covers.[18]

With the first verb, *has been copied*, Kagan doesn't reference who did the copying. But the context makes clear that other musicians were doing the copying. With the second verb phrase, Kagan names Dylan but deemphasizes his role by relegating him in a prepositional phrase. (Still, she also calls him "maybe rock's only Nobel Laureate and greatest-ever lyricist."[19])

That choice is intentional. Kagan's dissent criticizes the majority for disregarding the commonplace nature of artists copying other artists. She turns the reader's attention to the copying, not the copier.

Good writers know how to spot passive voice—and change their wording to active voice when it works better. Kagan could have written, "OK, you guessed it—Bob Dylan partly inspired *Rolling Stone*'s name." But that active wording lacks the same sharpness and detracts from her point.

Passive voice can appear in at least a dozen forms, depending on the verb tense and whether an optional prepositional phrase adds in the subject.

- His work **is / was copied** by other musicians.
- His work **is / was being copied** by other musicians.
- His work **had / has / must have / should have / would have / will have been copied**.

- His work **is going to be / will be / must be copied**.

In these next instances, the justices purposefully use passive voice verbs. They skip referencing the person or thing performing the action in a prepositional phrase. In this way, they focus on the action, rather than what's performing it.

- *Smith* **has been embattled** since the day it was decided, and calls for its reexamination **have intensified** in recent years.[20]
- Some of these individuals **have been reviled**; others **have been respected** as wise counselors.[21]
- The officers recognized from the scenery in the pictures that the elk **had been killed** in Bighorn and were able to locate the sites where the pictures **had been taken**.[22]

With these examples, it's unknown or unimportant who's doing the embattling and intensifying, the reviling and respecting, the killing and taking. The justices had another purpose. "Passive voice hides the relevant actor in plain sight," Barrett writes.[23] And when wielded purposefully by good writers, that's exactly the point.

32.5 Unanimous rule: Swap nominalizations for active verbs.

When judges take tough positions, they sometimes come out swinging—and they sometimes hold back. Compare how Justice Sotomayor criticizes the majority in these two dissents. In the first, she uses the more adamant, active verb *distorts*. In the second, she opts for the tamer nominalization, turning that verb into the noun *distortion*.

- Today, the Court **distorts** *Miller* and *Montgomery* beyond recognition.[24]
- The majority's overly broad reading of the tolling provision is thus unnecessary as well as a **distortion** of the clear statutory text.[25]

The first example is in a life-or-death case. Sotomayor is arguing against a life sentence for Brett Jones, who was 15 at the time of his crime. The second involves a 10-year sentence for a drug-related crime. Sotomayor switches between the active verb and the nominalization, depending on the seriousness of the case. As she shows, writers can back into or soften an argument by employing nominalizations, which turn active verbs into nouns or noun phrases.

But nominalizations make sentences wordier because they require additional verbs, articles, and prepositions. Nominalizations often crop up in sentences with weaker verbs and passive voice. Good writers avoid nominalizations, unless there's a purpose. When used, they should be a minor player in a sentence—as with an introductory clause or modifying phrase—rather than being paired with a weak verb to serve as the focal point. For instance, when addressing a series of points in the majority opinion, Thomas wrote, "I will **discuss** each in turn,"[26] not "I will **offer a discussion** of each point in turn."

Nominalizations typically end in -al (dismiss versus dismissal), -ance (guide, guidance), -ence (defer, deference), -ent (state, statement), -ion (object, objection), and -ity (apply, applicability). With nominalizations, the best practice is to downplay these nouns and pair them with more energetic main verbs, as shown here with *distills, underscores,* and *spar.*

- At the end of a lengthy **discussion,** the majority **distills** only this nugget: Congress's power over Indian affairs is "plenary" but not "absolute."[27]
- In my view, today's misguided foray **underscores** the wisdom of Congress's **decision** to create an agency that is uniquely positioned to evaluate the facts and apply the law in cases such as this one.[28]
- The parties **spar** over whether the government forfeited different **arguments** against district court jurisdiction premised on two provisions of the Administrative Procedure Act (APA).[29]

With nominalizations, the lesson is the same as with passive voice. Both make writing wordy and obtuse. When they appear in early drafts, good writers consider revising the prolix to the pithy—and make a conscious choice when opting for the former.

32.6 Unanimous rule: Generally, opt for dynamic verbs.

The most dynamic verbs stampede forward, as engines driving sentences. Others dash or putter. The most sluggish slink along like snails and include the *to be* verbs: *is, am, are, was, were, be, being,* and *been.* In a common editing drill, writers highlight all the *to be* verbs and transform them into dynamic ones. But as with many old-school writing rules, the justices don't follow this one absolutely.

This simplest verb can carry a sentence, especially when the words around it need simplifying or warrant a slowed pace. Here, Kagan shows her plain language prowess by keeping each subject flanking each *to be* verb:

- This case **is** about dog toys and whiskey, two items seldom appearing in the same sentence.[30]
- I **am** tempted merely to reply: Enough said about the majority's outlook on the statute before us.[31]
- And if you think **that's** just Shakespeare, here **are** a couple more.[32]
- And here it **was** so, the court found, because it "parodies" and "comments humorously" on Jack Daniel's.[33]
- Partisan gerrymandering of the kind before us not only subverts democracy (as if that **weren't** bad enough).[34]
- With that under your belt, you might **be** ready to absorb the relevant statutory language (but don't bet on it).[35]
- The current Court **is** textualist only when **being** so suits it.[36]

To be stands out as the quintessential static verb. These inert verbs describe a state of being, showing how one thinks or how things look, feel, or sound. Common static (or stative) verbs in legal writing include *agree* and *disagree, appear, believe, doubt, imagine, involve, know, prove, remain, seem, support,* and *think.*

Dynamic verbs, in contrast, propel the reader forward and give sentences momentum. Good storytellers prefer dynamic verbs because they show subjects in action and give life to narratives. Static verbs slow the reader down. Notice the distinct shift in cadence between the next two passages. In the first, Chief Justice Roberts uses static verbs to describe the Court's thinking. In the second, he spins a narrative and thrusts the reader into the story.

- This case, of course, does not **involve** "laying hands," but instead a shooting. Neither the parties nor the United States as *amicus curiae* **suggests** that the officers' use of bullets to restrain Torres alters the analysis in any way. And we are **aware** of no common law authority addressing an arrest under such circumstances, or indeed any case **involving** an application of force from a distance.[37]
- All told, the two officers **fired** 13 shots at Torres, **striking** her twice in the back and temporarily **paralyzing** her left arm. **Steering** with her right arm, Torres **accelerated** through the fusillade of bullets, **exited** the apartment complex, **drove** a short distance, and **stopped** in a parking lot. After **asking** a bystander **to report** an attempted carjacking, Torres **stole** a Kia Soul that **happened to be idling** nearby and **drove** 75 miles to Grants, New Mexico.[38]

Roberts shows that both types of verbs have a place in legal writing. Many sentences in opinions call for inert, static verbs so the justices can explain their rationales. But the justices don't shy away from stepping up their pace elsewhere. The justices employ dynamic verbs to energize their retelling of the facts and add spark to their analyses.

These dynamic verbs fall into two categories: transitive and intransitive verbs (and just to complicate matters further, some verbs can act as both). The distinction hasn't come up in Court opinions in more than a decade, and even then, only as a passing reference.[39]

In short, transitive verbs require a direct object—a noun, pronoun, or phrase that's essential to complete the sentence's meaning, explaining what the verb acts upon. Good writers keep those objects close—or closely understood—to their verbs. Justices Thomas, Kagan, Gorsuch, and Barrett show the best way here:

- Today's decision **distorts the record** of this case, **eviscerates our standard of review**, and **vacates four murder convictions** because the State struck a juror who would have been stricken by any competent attorney.[40]
- Well, no, **scratch that**.[41]
- Depending on how you **squint your eyes**, you **can stretch (or shrink) its meaning** to convict (or exonerate) just about anyone.[42]
- Florida **pins the collapse** on Georgia through a multistep causal chain.[43]

Intransitive verbs are the opposite. They don't make sense with objects. Adverbs, prepositional phrases, and other modifying clauses can follow intransitive verbs to add meaning, typically showing where, when, how, or how long something happened. Again here, the best writers keep those modifying words and phrases close.

- From top to bottom, the analysis **fails**.[44]
- Meanwhile, the suspect **may stroll** into the home and then **dash** out the back door.[45]
- Those safeguards **would apply or not apply**, or **fluctuate** constantly between the two, based on the happenstance of whether Medicare paid for hospital care on a given day.[46]
- The greater likelihood of confusion **inheres** in the latter use, because it is the one conveying information (or misinformation) about who is responsible for a product.[47]
- Later in 2016, however, Mr. Talevski's condition suddenly **deteriorated**.[48]

Some verbs can act as either transitive or intransitive, meaning they work with or without an object. The verb *to drive* can be transitive because a police officer can literally drive a car or a judge's analysis could figuratively drive a reversal. But it can also be intransitive, as in *an officer drives* or *an officer drives to the suspect's home*. Other switch-hitters include *read, understand*, and *return*.

- The Executive therefore cannot unilaterally **return these migrants** to Mexico.[49] (transitive)
- Today, the Court **returns to these quandaries**.[50] (intransitive)

The takeaway is that some verbs require help, in the form of objects, prepositions, and modifying clauses. But sometimes that help is a crutch for weak writing, disguised in wordy verb phrases, passive voice, and nominalizations. Words clinging to verbs can often be cut to create a more dynamic sentence. A good writer would cut more than half of the verbs and verb phrases from this first example to create the second:

- After proceedings before the agency **had come to a conclusion**, the FDIC **went ahead and issued an order that resulted in the removal of petitioner from office**, the **prohibition of further banking activities by him** and the **issuing of an assessment** of $125,000 in civil penalties.

Revised:

- After proceedings before the agency **concluded**, the FDIC **ordered** petitioner removed from office, **prohibited** him from further banking activities, and **assessed** $125,000 in civil penalties.[51]

Closing

A brighter future is ours to write. Let's begin this new chapter—
together—and let's start the work right now.[1]

—President Barack Obama

Good writers slash excess. They prune anything that doesn't add meaning to a sentence, cutting whatever goes beyond the intended point. Chief Justice Roberts has repeatedly praised *Brown v. Board of Education* for achieving that balance, noting it's a fraction of the lengthier opinions of today. He explained that Chief Justice Earl Warren cut *Brown* to a mere 10 pages because "Warren knew that if he wrote another sentence, the unanimous consensus he had would start to fall apart."[2]

Roberts said that brevity had a cost: "The price was he didn't resolve all the issues that were going to come forward. You can reasonably debate, 'should he have issued a 5–4 opinion that's 80-pages long and settled all these issues?' And he decided, 'no,' he was going to announce the basic principle, let it go, and then it would take generations to resolve all the subordinate issues."[3]

Letting go is perhaps the hardest gamble for any writer. Roberts has called *Brown* "probably the greatest decision of the Supreme Court since *Marbury v. Madison*."[4] Warren wrapped up *Brown* with just 10 memorable pages, cementing it with this enduring line—one with unassuming verbs and enduring authority that made a vital mark on history: "We conclude that in the field of public education the doctrine of 'separate but equal' has no place."[5]

And with that, it's time to let go of this book, with this final advice: Be bold, writers. Go make your mark. Your place in history is now.

Notes

All opinions can be found at https://www.supremecourt.gov/opinions or by searching the case name at https://www.oyez.org/. Citations are omitted from opinions for readability. Any bold font is this author's emphasis. For more, go to jillbarton.net.

INTRODUCTION: A SUPREME WRITING REVOLUTION

1. The Declaration of Independence para. 2 (U.S. 1776) (Capitalization omitted: At the time, writers followed the German practice of capitalizing nouns.).
2. U.S. Const. amends. I, IV.
3. U.S. Const. amend. XIV.
4. Zachary Crockett, *The Most Expensive Typo in Legislative History*, Priceonomics (Oct. 9, 2014), https://priceonomics.com/the-most-expensive-typo-in-legislative-history/.
5. Livia Albeck-Ripka, *Missing Apostrophe in Facebook Post Lands a Man in Defamation Court*, N.Y. Times, Oct. 11, 2021, at A8.
6. Justin Jouvenal, *A 12-Year-Old Girl Is Facing Criminal Charges for Using Certain Emoji*, Wash. Post (Feb. 27, 2016), https://www.washingtonpost.com/news/local/wp/2016/02/27/a-12-year-old-girl-is-facing-criminal-charges-for-using-emoji-shes-not-alone/.
7. Me. Stat. tit. 26 § 664(3)(F) (2018); *Maine Legislative Drafting Manual* 113 (Leg. Council, Maine State Leg. 2009), http://maine.gov/legis/ros/manual/Draftman2009.pdf.
8. Daniel Victor, *Suit Over Oxford Comma Is Settled*, N.Y. Times, Feb. 10, 2018, at A11.
9. Alex Carp, *Writing with Antonin Scalia*, New Yorker (July 16, 2012), https://www.newyorker.com/news/news-desk/writing-with-antonin-scalia-grammar-nerd.
10. *Obergefell v. Hodges*, 576 U.S. 644, 720 (2015) (Scalia, J., dissenting).

CHAPTER 1

1. Oliver Wendell Holmes, *Medical Essays* 377 (Houghton-Mifflin 1909). The original quote, "[t]he young man knows the rules, but the old man knows the exceptions," is updated to reflect modern conventions.
2. Editorial, *Was Jane Austen Edited?*, NPR (Nov. 17, 2010), https://www.npr.org/2010/11/15/131335890/was-jane-austen-edited-does-it-matter; *Word History: Why Do We Use Apostrophes?*, Merriam-Webster.com, https://www.merriam-webster.com/words-at-play/history-and-use-of-the-apostrophe.
3. Apostrophe Protection Society, http://www.apostrophe.org.uk/.
4. *King v. Burwell*, 576 U.S. 473, 513 (2015) (Scalia, J., dissenting) ("If that is so, however, **wouldn't** one expect States to react by setting up their own Exchanges? And **wouldn't** that outcome satisfy two of the Act's goals . . .?").
5. Kavanaugh has done so only once recently. *Ramirez v. Collier*, 595 U.S. 411, 443 (2022) (Kavanaugh, J., concurring).
6. The original line is "When you ain't got nothing, you got nothing to lose." *Sprint Commc'ns Co., L.P. v. APCC Servs., Inc.*, 554 U.S. 269, 301 (2008) (Roberts, C.J., dissenting).
7. University of Minn., *2018 Stein Lecture: John G. Roberts, Jr., Chief Justice of the United States*, YouTube, at 34:44 (Oct. 6, 2018), https://www.youtube.com/watch?v=9i3RwWoy_kE.
8. *Burwell v. Hobby Lobby Stores, Inc.*, 573 U.S. 682, 770 (2014) (Ginsburg, J., dissenting).
9. *Dunn v. Ray*, 139 S. Ct. 661, 662 (2019) (Kagan, J., dissenting).
10. *Moore v. Texas*, 139 S. Ct. 666, 672 (2019) (Roberts, C.J., concurring).
11. *Seila Law LLC v. CFPB*, 140 S. Ct. 2183, 2207 (2020) (Roberts, C.J.).
12. *June Med. Servs. LLC v. Russo*, 140 S. Ct. 2103, 2126 (2020) (Breyer, J.).
13. *New Prime Inc. v. Oliveira*, 139 S. Ct. 532, 539 (2019) (Gorsuch, J.).
14. *303 Creative LLC v. Elenis*, 600 U.S. 570, 640 (2023) (Sotomayor, J., dissenting).
15. *Henson v. Santander Cons. USA Inc.*, 582 U.S. 79, 81 (2017) (Gorsuch, J.).
16. *See, e.g.*, the unanimous *Dawson v. Steager*, 139 S. Ct. 698, 704 (2019), where Justice Gorsuch used 13 contractions and two in one sentence: "Yet that **wasn't** enough to save the state statutes in *Davis*, *Barker*, or *Phillips*, and it **can't** be enough here."
17. *Bostock v. Clayton Cnty.*, 590 U.S. 644, 676 (2020) (Gorsuch, J.).
18. Livia Albeck-Ripka, *Missing Apostrophe in Facebook Post Lands a Man in Defamation Court*, N.Y. Times, Oct. 11, 2021, at A8 (emphasis added) (cleaned up).

19. *Taylor v. United States*, 579 U.S. 301, 307 (2016) (quoting *Gonzales v. Reich*, 545 U.S. 1, 17 (2005)). Sotomayor also did so in a paragraph: "Even so, the court held that **Congress'** appropriations riders impliedly 'repealed or suspended' the Government's obligation. . . . [T]he panel . . . found that the riders here 'adequately expressed **Congress's** intent . . . .'" *Me. Cmty. Health Options v. United States*, 140 S. Ct. 1308, 1318 (2020) (quoting *Moda Health Plan, Inc. v. United States*, 892 F.3d 1311, 1322–23, 1325 (Fed. Cir. 2018)).

20. *See, e.g., Barton v. Barr*, 140 S. Ct. 1442, 1453 (2020) (Kavanaugh, J.) ("**Congress'** intent"); *Babcock v. Kijakazi*, 595 U.S. 77, 84 (2022) (Barrett, J.) ("**Congress'** choice").

21. *Atl. Richfield Co. v. Christian*, 140 S. Ct. 1335, 1362 (2020) (Gorsuch, J., concurring and dissenting).

22. *Kahler v. Kansas*, 140 S. Ct. 1021, 1031 (2020) (Kagan, J.).

23. *Lamps Plus, Inc., v. Varela*, 139 S. Ct. 1407, 1413 (2019) (Roberts, C. J.).

24. *Biestek v. Berryhill*, 139 S. Ct. 1148, 1161 (2019) (Gorsuch, J., dissenting).

25. *Kahler*, 140 S. Ct. at 1038 (Breyer, J., dissenting).

26. *Cnty. of Maui v. Haw. Wildlife Fund*, 140 S. Ct. 1462, 1478 (2020) (Kavanaugh, J., concurring).

27. *Fort Bend Cnty. v. Davis*, 139 S. Ct. 1843, 1847 (2019) (Ginsburg, J.).

28. *Barton*, 140 S. Ct. at 1451 (Kavanaugh, J.).

29. *Cedar Point Nursery v. Hassid*, 141 S. Ct. 2063, 2086 (2021) (Breyer, J., dissenting).

30. *Niz-Chavez v. Garland*, 593 U.S. 155, 159 (Gorsuch, J.).

31. *Wash. State Dep't of Licensing v. Cougar Den, Inc.*, 139 S. Ct. 1000, 1019 (2019) (Gorsuch, J., concurring) (emphasis omitted).

32. *Dawson*, 139 S. Ct. at 702 (Gorsuch, J.).

33. *Apple Inc. v. Pepper*, 139 S. Ct. 1514, 1523 (2019) (Kavanaugh, J.).

34. *Home Depot USA, Inc. v. Jackson*, 139 S. Ct. 1743, 1752 (2019) (Alito, J., dissenting).

35. *Timbs v. Indiana*, 139 S. Ct. 682, 688 (2019) (Ginsburg, J.).

36. *Shurtleff v. Boston*, 596 U.S. 243, 279 (2022) (Gorsuch, J., concurring).

37. *Andy Warhol Found. for the Visual Arts, Inc. v. Goldsmith*, 598 U.S. 508, 557 (2023) (Gorsuch, J., concurring).

38. *Bostock*, 590 U.S. at 711 (Alito, J., dissenting) (quoting GAO, Security Clearances, at 2).

39. *June Med. Servs. LLC*, 140 S. Ct. at 2125 (Breyer, J.).

40. *Dobbs v. Jackson Women's Health Org.*, 597 U.S. 215, 231 (2022) (Alito, J.).

41. *Allen v. Milligan*, 599 U.S. 1, 90 (2023) (Thomas, J., dissenting).

42. *Seila Law LLC*, 140 S. Ct. at 2240 (Kagan, J., concurring in judgment and dissenting in part).

CHAPTER 2

1. *Niz-Chavez v. Garland*, 593 U.S. 155, 162 (2021).
2. *Sturgeon v. Frost*, 587 U.S. 28, 47 (2019) (Kagan, J.).
3. *Nieves v. Bartlett*, 139 S. Ct. 1715, 1721 (2019) (Roberts, C. J.).
4. *Allen v. Milligan*, 599 U.S. 1, 37 (2023) (Roberts, C. J.).
5. *Our Lady of Guadalupe Sch. v. Morrissey-Berru*, 140 S. Ct. 2049, 2078 (2020) (Sotomayor, J., dissenting).
6. *Thacker v. Tenn. Valley Auth.*, 139 S. Ct. 1435, 1441 (2019) (Kagan, J.).
7. *Dobbs v. Jackson Women's Health Org.*, 597 U.S. 215, 402 (2022) (Breyer, Sotomayor, Kagan, JJ., dissenting).
8. *Nieves*, 139 S. Ct. at 1725 (Roberts, C. J.).
9. *Madison v. Alabama*, 139 S. Ct. 718, 723–24 (2019) (Kagan, J.).
10. *Fulton v. Philadelphia*, 593 U.S. 522, 572 n.37 (2021) (Alito, J. concurring).
11. *Garza v. Idaho*, 139 S. Ct. 738, 743 n.2 (2019) (Sotomayor, J.).

CHAPTER 3

1. AALS, *A Conversation with Justice Sonia Sotomayor*, YouTube, at 56:00 (Jan. 4, 2023), https://www.youtube.com/watch?v=WU3vFuCg920.
2. Adam Calhoun, *Punctuation in Novels*, Medium (Feb. 15, 2016), https://medium.com/@neuroecology/punctuation-in-novels-8f316d542ec4#.iy5tosbhv.
3. The 121-word sentence begins: "Her antiquity in preceding and surviving succeeding tellurian generations: her nocturnal predominance: her satellitic dependence: her luminary reflection: her constancy . . . ." James Joyce, *Ulysses* 1841 (Duke 2012).
4. *See, e.g.*, William Strunk Jr. and E. B. White, *The Elements of Style* 7–8 (4th ed. 2000) ("Use a colon after an independent clause to introduce a list . . . .").
5. *See, e.g., id.* at 8.
6. *Madison v. Alabama*, 139 S. Ct. 718, 724 (2019) (Kagan, J.).
7. *Weyerhaeuser Co. v. FWS*, 139 S. Ct. 361, 365 (2018) (Roberts, C. J.).
8. *Delaware v. Pennsylvania*, 598 U.S. 115, 136 (2023) (Jackson, J.).
9. *Home Depot USA, Inc. v. Jackson*, 139 S. Ct. 1743, 1756 (2019) (Alito, J., dissenting).
10. *Wash. State Dep't of Licensing v. Cougar Den, Inc.*, 139 S. Ct. 1000, 1019 (2019) (Gorsuch, J., concurring).
11. *Ams. for Prosperity Found. v. Bonta*, 141 S. Ct. 2373, 2398 n.5 (2021) (Sotomayor, J., dissenting).

12. *See, e.g.*, Strunk and White, 7–8 ("Use a colon after an independent clause to introduce a list . . . . [A colon] should not separate a verb from its complement or a preposition from its object.").

13. *Fin. Oversight & Mgmt. Bd. for P.R. v. Aurelius Inv., LLC*, 140 S. Ct. 1649, 1662 (2020) (Breyer, J.).

14. *Garza v. Idaho*, 139 S. Ct. 738, 752 (2019) (Thomas, J., dissenting).

15. *Cnty. of Maui v. Haw. Wildlife Fund*, 140 S. Ct. 1462, 1485 (2020) (Alito, J., dissenting).

16. *Cougar Den, Inc.*, 139 S. Ct. at 1025 (Roberts, C. J., dissenting).

CHAPTER 4

1. BU School of Law, *Commencement 2023: Supreme Court Justice Ketanji Brown Jackson*, YouTube, at 23:51 (May 22, 2023), https://www.youtube.com/watch?v=idUqcMItAWo.

2. *See, e.g.*, Christina Sterbenz, *This Comma Cost America About $40 Million*, Bus. Insider (Jan. 9, 2015), http://www.businessinsider.com/this-typo-cost-america-about-40-million-2015-1.

3. *See, e.g.*, *O'Connor v. Oakhurst Dairy*, No. 16-1901, 2017 WL 957195, at *2 (1st Cir. Mar. 13, 2017) (a missing serial comma in a state law listing overtime exemptions cost a Maine dairy company $5 million); *Rogers Cable Commc'ns Inc. v. Bell Aliant*, Telecom Decision CRTC 2006-45, rev'd, Telecom Decision CRTC 2007-75.

4. *See, e.g.*, Patrick Finglass, *A Comma in Catullus* (Aug. 15, 2015), https://blog.oup.com/2015/08/a-comma-in-catullus/.

5. Bryan A. Garner, *Interview with Chief Justice John G Roberts, Jr.*, 13 Scribes J. of Leg. Writing 5, 40 (2010).

6. *Weyerhaeuser Co. v. FWS*, 139 S. Ct. 361, 365 (2018) (Roberts, C. J.).

7. *Nieves v. Bartlett*, 139 S. Ct. 1715, 1720 (2019) (Roberts, C. J.).

8. *Nieves*, 139 S. Ct. at 1737 (Sotomayor, J. dissenting).

9. *Obduskey v. McCarthy & Holthus LLP*, 139 S. Ct. 1029, 1040 (2019) (Breyer, J.).

10. *Apple Inc. v. Pepper*, 139 S. Ct. 1514, 1519 (2019) (Kavanaugh, J.).

11. *BNSF R. Co. v. Loos*, 139 S. Ct. 893, 902 n.4 (2019) (Ginsburg, J.).

12. *Nieves*, 139 S. Ct. at 1720 (Roberts, C. J.).

13. *See, e.g.*, Plain Writing Tips, https://www.archives.gov/open/plain-writing/tips/commas.html; William Strunk Jr. and E. B. White, *The Elements of Style* 5 (4th ed. 2000) ("When the subject is the same for both clauses and is expressed only once, a comma is useful if the connective is *but*. When the connective is *and*, the comma

should be omitted if the relation between the two clauses is close or immediate.").

14. *Nieves*, 139 S. Ct. at 1721 (Roberts, C. J.).

15. *Id.*

16. *United States v. Haymond*, 139 S. Ct. 2369, 2380 (2019) (Gorsuch, J.). While it's rare for the justices to use a comma with "and" in a dependent clause, all do so. When in doubt, the best bet is to opt against a comma.

17. *Nieves*, 139 S. Ct. at 1720 (Roberts, C. J.).

18. *Fourth Est. Pub. Benefit Corp. v. Wall-Street.com, LLC*, 139 S. Ct. 881, 887 (2019) (Ginsburg, J.).

19. *Allen v. Cooper*, 589 U.S. 248, 268 (2020) (Thomas, J., concurring).

20. *CITGO Asphalt Ref. Co. v. Frescati Shipping Co., Ltd.*, 140 S. Ct. 1081, 1090 (2020) (Sotomayor, J.).

21. *Andy Warhol Found. for the Visual Arts, Inc. v. Goldsmith*, 598 U.S. 508, 542 (2023) (Sotomayor, J.).

22. *United States ex rel. Schutte v. SuperValu Inc.*, 598 U.S. 739, 747 (2023) (Thomas, J.).

23. *See, e.g.*, Anne Enquist et al., *Just Writing: Grammar, Punctuation, and Style for the Legal Writer* Rule 9.1(2) (5th ed. 2017) ("Use A Comma To Set Off Long Introductory Clauses . . . .").

24. *Biestek v. Berryhill*, 139 S. Ct. 1148, 1161 (2019) (Gorsuch, J., dissenting).

25. *Air & Liquid Sys. Corp. v. DeVries*, 586 U.S. 446, 464 (2019) (Gorsuch, J., dissenting).

26. *BNSF R. Co.*, 139 S. Ct. at 905 (Gorsuch, J. dissenting).

27. *Box v. Planned Parenthood of Ind. & Ky., Inc.*, 139 S. Ct. 1780, 1788 (2019) (Thomas, J., concurring).

28. *Herrera v. Wyoming*, 139 S. Ct. 1686, 1701 (2019) (Sotomayor, J.).

29. *Dawson v. Steager*, 139 S. Ct. 698, 703 (2019) (Gorsuch, J.).

30. *Bucklew v. Precythe*, 139 S. Ct. 1112, 1120 (2019) (Gorsuch, J.).

31. *Id.* at 1124.

32. *Nieves*, 139 S. Ct. at 1720 (Roberts, C. J.).

33. *Bucklew*, 139 S. Ct. at 1120-21 (Gorsuch, J.).

34. *Home Depot USA, Inc. v. Jackson*, 139 S. Ct. 1743, 1753 (2019) (Alito, J., dissenting).

35. *Wash. State Dep't of Licensing v. Cougar Den, Inc.*, 139 S. Ct. 1000, 1008 (2019) (Breyer, J.).

36. *Smith v. Berryhill*, 139 S. Ct. 1765, 1771–72 (2019) (Sotomayor, J.).

37. *Cougar Den, Inc.*, 139 S. Ct. at 1023 (Roberts, C. J., dissenting).

38. *Sturgeon v. Frost*, 587 U.S. 28, 44 (2019) (Kagan, J.).

39. *Republic of Sudan v. Harrison*, 139 S. Ct. 1048, 1054–55 (2019) (Alito, J.).

40. *BNSF R. Co.*, 139 S. Ct. at 900 (Ginsburg, J.).

41. *Madison v. Alabama*, 139 S. Ct. 718, 726 (2019) (Kagan, J.).

42. *Nieves*, 139 S. Ct. at 1720 (Roberts, C. J.).

43. *Id.* at 1730 (Gorsuch, J., concurring and dissenting).

44. *Mont v. United States*, 139 S. Ct. 1826, 1838 (2019) (Sotomayor, J., dissenting).

45. *Id.* at 1830 (Thomas, J.).

46. *Gamble v. United States*, 139 S. Ct. 1960, 1964 (2019) (Alito, J.).

47. *Stokeling v. United States*, 139 S. Ct. 544, 549 (2019) (Thomas, J.).

48. *Jam v. Int'l Fin. Corp.*, 139 S. Ct. 759, 765 (2019) (Roberts, C. J.).

49. Interview with Roberts, 13 Scribes J. Legal Writing at 38.

50. *Allen v. Milligan*, 599 U.S. 1, 17 (2023) (Roberts, C. J.).

51. *Id.* at 11.

52. *BNSF R. Co.*, 139 S. Ct. at 897 (Ginsburg, J.).

53. *Fourth Est. Pub. Benefit Corp.*, 139 S. Ct. at 887 (Ginsburg, J.).

54. *Nielsen v. Preap*, 139 S. Ct. 954, 961 (2019) (Alito, J.).

55. *Nieves*, 139 S. Ct. at 1720 (Roberts, C. J.).

56. *Madison*, 139 S. Ct. at 723 (Kagan, J.).

57. *Return Mail, Inc. v. USPS*, 139 S. Ct. 1853, 1859 (2019) (Sotomayor, J.).

58. *Home Depot USA, Inc.*, 139 S. Ct. at 1755 (Alito, J., dissenting).

59. *Biden v. Nebraska*, 600 U.S. 477, 541 (2023) (Kagan, J., dissenting).

60. Interview with Roberts, 13 Scribes J. Legal Writing at 38.

61. *Weyerhaeuser Co.*, 139 S. Ct. at 369 (Roberts, C. J.).

62. *Cougar Den, Inc.*, 139 S. Ct. at 1026 (Roberts, C. J., dissenting).

63. *Nieves*, 139 S. Ct. at 1725 (Roberts, C. J.).

64. *Id.* at 1720.

65. *Weyerhaeuser Co.*, 139 S. Ct. at 365 (Roberts, C. J.).

66. *Atl. Richfield Co. v. Christian*, 140 S. Ct. 1335, 1347–48 (2020) (Roberts, C. J.).

67. *McGirt v. Oklahoma*, 140 S. Ct. 2452, 2482 (2020) (Roberts, C. J., dissenting).

68. *Trump v. Mazars USA, LLP*, 591 U.S. 848, 853 (2020) (Roberts, C. J.).

CHAPTER 5

1. *Chicago v. Env't Def. Fund*, 511 U.S. 328, 335 n.1 (1994).

2. *Fin. Oversight & Mgmt. Bd. for P. R. v. Aurelius Inv., LLC*, 140 S. Ct. 1649, 1664 (2020) (Breyer, J.).

3. *Palmore v. United States*, 411 U.S. 389, 407 (1973).

4. *Students for Fair Admissions, Inc. v. President & Fellows of Harvard Coll.*, 600 U.S. 181, 213 (2023) (Roberts, C.J.).
5. *Jones v. Hendrix*, 599 U.S. 465, 485 (2023) (Thomas, J.).
6. *Bartlett v. Nieves*, 712 F. App'x 613, 615 (9th Cir. 2017).
7. *Nieves v. Bartlett*, 139 S. Ct. 1715, 1728 (Roberts, C.J.).
8. Oral Argument at 4:07, *Moore v. Harper*, 600 U.S. 1 (2023), https://www.oyez.org/cases/2022/21-1271.
9. *Moore v. Harper*, 600 U.S. 1, 37 (2023) (Roberts, C.J.).
10. *Mitchell v. Wisconsin*, 139 S. Ct. 2525, 2536 (2019) (Alito, J.).
11. *Andy Warhol Found. for the Visual Arts, Inc. v. Goldsmith*, 598 U.S. 508, 523 (2023) (Sotomayor, J.).
12. *Id.* at 528.

CHAPTER 6

1. *West Virginia v. EPA*, 597 U.S. 697, 756 (2022) (Kagan, J., dissenting).
2. *See, e.g.,* Noreen Malone, *The Case—Please Hear Me Out—Against the Em Dash*, Slate (May 24, 2011), https://slate.com/human-interest/2011/05/em-dashes-why-writers-should-use-them-more-sparingly.html; Philip B. Corbett, *Dashes Everywhere*, N.Y. Times (April 5, 2011), https://afterdeadline.blogs.nytimes.com/2011/04/05/dashes-everywhere/.
3. *Knick v. Twp. of Scott*, 588 U.S. 180, 220 (2019) (Kagan, J., dissenting).
4. *Am. Legion v. Am. Humanist Ass'n*, 139 S. Ct. 2067, 2075 (2019) (Alito, J.).
5. *Allen v. Cooper*, 589 U.S. 248, 256 (2020) (Kagan, J.).
6. *Weyerhaeuser Co. v. FWS*, 139 S. Ct. 361, 364–65 (2018) (Roberts, C.J.).
7. *Allen*, 589 U.S. at 263 (Kagan, J.).

CHAPTER 7

1. *W. Va. Bd. of Educ. v. Barnette*, 319 U.S. 624, 632–33 (1943).
2. Bryan A. Garner, *Interview with Justice Antonin Scalia*, 13 Scribes J. of Leg. Writing 51, 64 (2010).
3. *United States v. Ballenger*, No. CR 21-719 (JEB), 2023 WL 4581846, at *6 (D.D.C. July 18, 2023).
4. *Id.* at *11.
5. *United States v. Cochran*, 534 F.3d 631, 635 (7th Cir. 2008).
6. *Commonwealth v. Castano*, 82 N.E.3d 974, 978 (Mass. 2017).
7. Justin Jouvenal, *A 12-Year-Old Girl Is Facing Criminal Charges for Using Certain Emoji*, Wash. Post (Feb. 27, 2016), https://www.washingtonpost.

com/news/local/wp/2016/02/27/a-12-year-old-girl-is-facing-crimi
nal-charges-for-using-emoji-shes-not-alone/.

8. William Strunk Jr. and E. B. White haven't updated their *The Elements
   of Style* (originally published in 1918) since 1979. Later updates were
   published posthumously.

9. *Mahanoy Area Sch. Dist. v. B. L.*, 141 S. Ct. 2038, 2043 (2021) (Breyer,
   J.) ("The second image was blank but for a caption, which read: 'Love
   how me and [another student] get told we need a year of jv before we
   make varsity but tha[t] doesn't matter to anyone else?' The caption also
   contained an upside-down smiley-face emoji.").

10. *People in Int. of R.D*, 464 P.3d 717, 730 (Colo. 2020).

11. *Ghanam v. Does*, 845 N.W.2d 128, 145 (Mich. Ct. App. 2014).

CHAPTER 8

1. *303 Creative LLC v. Elenis*, 600 U.S. 570, 634 (2023) (Sotomayor, J.,
   dissenting).

2. Dinitia Smith, *Fine Points of Dashes Set Heads Spinning*, N.Y. Times, Aug.
   7, 2003, at E1.

3. *Brnovich v. DNC*, 141 S. Ct. 2321, 2367 (2021) (Kagan, J., dissenting).

4. *Espinoza v. Mont. Dep't of Rev.*, 140 S. Ct. 2246, 2269 n.2 (2020) (Alito, J.,
   concurring).

5. *Jones v. Mississippi*, 593 U.S. 98, 101 (2021) (Kavanaugh, J.).

6. *Kansas v. Garcia*, 140 S. Ct. 791, 797 (2020) (Alito, J.).

CHAPTER 9

1. Bryan A. Garner, *Interview with Justice Stephen Breyer*, 13 Scribes J. of Leg.
   Writing 145, 156 (2010).

2. *See, e.g.*, William R. Domnarski, *The Urge to Exclaim*, Daily J. (Sept.
   2, 2014), https://www.dailyjournal.com/articles/324291-the-urge-to-
   exclaim.

3. Elmore Leonard, *Ten Rules of Writing* 33 (2007). Leonard added, referencing *The Bonfire of the Vanities'* author: "If you have the knack of playing
   with exclaimers the way Tom Wolfe does, you can throw them in by the
   handful."

4. *Rehaif v. United States*, 139 S. Ct. 2191, 2204 (2019) (Alito, J., dissenting).

5. *Andrus v. Texas*, 140 S. Ct. 1875, 1888 (2020) (Alito, J., dissenting).

6. *Brnovich v. DNC*, 141 S. Ct. 2321, 2361 n.7 (2021) (Kagan, J., dissenting).

7. *Dobbs v. Jackson Women's Health Org.*, 597 U.S. 215, 371 (2022) (Breyer, Sotomayor, Kagan, JJ., dissenting).

8. See more on how punctuation fits with quotations in section 14.6.2.

9. *Sturgeon v. Frost*, 587 U.S. 28, 36 (2019) (Kagan, J.).

10. *Students for Fair Admissions, Inc. v. President & Fellows of Harvard Coll.*, 600 U.S. 181, 384 (2023) (Sotomayor, J., dissenting).

CHAPTER 10

1. *Entergy Corp. v. Riverkeeper, Inc.*, 556 U.S. 208, 220 n.6 (2009).

2. Bryan A. Garner, *Interview with Justice Antonin Scalia*, 13 Scribes J. of Leg. Writing 51, 63 (2010).

3. *Id.*

4. *United States v. Davis*, 139 S. Ct. 2319, 2326 (2019) (Gorsuch, J.) (quoting *Sessions v. Dimaya*, 138 S. Ct. 1204, 1216 (2018) (Kagan, J.)).

5. *Dep't of Com. v. New York*, 139 S. Ct. 2551, 2582 (2019) (Thomas, J., concurring in part and dissenting in part).

6. *Vega v. Tekoh*, 597 U.S. 134, 155 (2022) (Kagan, J., dissenting).

7. *Barr v. Am. Ass'n of Pol. Consultants, Inc.*, 140 S. Ct. 2335, 2345 (2020) (Kavanaugh, J.).

8. *The Supreme Court's Style Guide* lists Webster's Third New International Dictionary as the "general authority" and lists hyphenated and non-hyphenated words. S. Ct. Style G. §§ 4.1–4.3 (2016).

9. *Davis*, 139 S. Ct. at 2338 (Kavanaugh, J., dissenting).

10. *Abitron Austria GmbH v. Hetronic Int'l, Inc.*, 600 U.S. 412, 439 (2023) (Sotomayor, J., concurring).

11. *June Med. Servs. LLC v. Russo*, 140 S. Ct. 2103, 2112 (2020) (Breyer, J.).

12. *Am. Legion v. Am. Humanist Ass'n*, 139 S. Ct. 2067, 2102 (2019) (Gorsuch, J., concurring).

13. *Allen v. Milligan*, 599 U.S. 1, 47 (2023) (Thomas, J., dissenting).

14. *Davis*, 139 S Ct. at 2333 (Gorsuch, J.).

15. *Am. Legion*, 139 S. Ct. at 2077 (Alito, J.).

16. *Trump v. Mazars USA, LLP*, 591 U.S. 848, 859 (2020) (Roberts, C. J.).

17. *Espinoza v. Mont. Dep't of Rev.*, 140 S. Ct. 2246, 2253 (2020) (Roberts, C. J.) ("The Montana Supreme Court acknowledged that 'an overly-broad' application . . . .").

18. *Little Sisters Poor Saints Peter & Paul Home v. Pennsylvania*, 140 S. Ct. 2367, 2388 (2020) (Alito, J., concurring).

19. *Rucho v. Common Cause*, 139 S. Ct. 2484, 2511 (2019) (Kagan, J., dissenting).

20. *Glacier Nw., Inc., v. Teamsters*, 598 U.S. 771, 797 (2023) (Jackson, J., dissenting).
21. *Mahanoy Area Sch. Dist. v. B. L.*, 141 S. Ct. 2038, 2044 (2021) (Breyer, J.).
22. *Am. Ass'n of Pol. Consultants, Inc.*, 140 S. Ct. at 2359 (Breyer, J., concurring and dissenting).

CHAPTER 11

1. *United States v. Woods*, 571 U.S. 31, 45 (2013).
2. Ruth Bader Ginsburg, *My Own Words* 12 (2016).
3. Vladimir Nabokov, *Lolita* 10 (Vintage 1989).
4. *Jack Daniel's Props., Inc. v. VIP Prods. LLC*, 599 U.S. 140, 145 (2023) (Kagan, J.).
5. *Borden v. United States*, 593 U.S. 420, 437 (2021) (Kagan, J.).
6. *Bostock v. Clayton Cnty.*, 590 U.S. 644, 666 (2020) (Gorsuch, J.).
7. *Chiafalo v. Washington*, 591 U.S. 578, 582 (2020) (Kagan, J.).
8. *Id.* at 583.
9. *Bostock*, 590 U.S. at 668–69 (Gorsuch, J.).
10. *Air & Liquid Sys. Corp. v. DeVries*, 586 U.S. 446, 450 (2019) (Kavanaugh, J.).
11. *Timbs v. Indiana*, 139 S. Ct. 682, 689 (2019) (Ginsburg, J.).
12. *Biestek v. Berryhill*, 139 S. Ct. 1148, 1153 (2019) (Kagan, J.).

CHAPTER 12

1. *Moore v. Harper*, 600 U.S. 1, 55 (2023) (Thomas, J., dissenting).
2. *Dutra Grp. v. Batterton*, 588 U.S. 358, 386 (2019) (Ginsburg, J., dissenting).
3. *Pennsylvania v. Dunlap*, 555 U.S. 964, 964 (2008) (Roberts, C. J., dissenting).
4. *King v. Burwell*, 576 U.S. 473, 507 (2015) (Scalia, J., dissenting).
5. *Axon Enter., Inc. v. FTC*, 598 U.S. 175, 206 (2023) (Gorsuch, J., concurring).
6. *Allen v. Cooper*, 589 U.S. 248, 252 (2020) (Kagan, J.).
7. *USFS v. Cowpasture River Pres. Ass'n*, 140 S. Ct. 1837, 1860 (2020) (Sotomayor, J., dissenting).
8. *Jack Daniel's Props., Inc. v. VIP Prods. LLC*, 599 U.S. 140, 144 (2023) (Kagan, J.).
9. *CITGO Asphalt Ref. Co. v. Frescati Shipping Co., Ltd.*, 140 S. Ct. 1081, 1095 (2020) (Thomas, J., dissenting).
10. *Rucho v. Common Cause*, 139 S. Ct. 2484, 2509 (2019) (Kagan, J., dissenting).

11. *Andy Warhol Found. for the Visual Arts, Inc. v. Goldsmith*, 598 U.S. 508, 558–59 (2023) (Kagan, J., dissenting).
12. *Bostock v. Clayton Cnty.*, 590 U.S. 644, 661 (2020) (Gorsuch, J.).
13. *Id.* at 788 (Kavanaugh, J., dissenting).

CHAPTER 13

1. John Hockenberry, *Interview with Justice Ruth Bader Ginsburg*, The World (Sept. 16, 2013), https://theworld.org/stories/2013-09-16/transcript-interview-supreme-court-justice-ruth-bader-ginsburg.
2. *Nat'l Pork Producers Council v. Ross*, 598 U.S. 356, 363 (2023) (Gorsuch, J.).
3. Paul A. Freund, *Charles Evans Hughes As Chief Justice*, 81 Harv. L. Rev. 4, 37 (1967) (citing Hughes, *Address to ALI*, 22 A.B.A.J. 374, 375 (1936)).
4. *Dubin v. United States*, 599 U.S. 110, 136 (2023) (Gorsuch, J., concurring).
5. *Cnty. of Maui v. Haw. Wildlife Fund*, 140 S. Ct. 1462, 1470 (2020) (Breyer, J.).
6. See more on how punctuation fits with quotations in section 14.6.2.
7. *Kahler v. Kansas*, 140 S. Ct. 1021, 1040 (2020) (Breyer, J., dissenting).

CHAPTER 14

1. *United States v. Haymond*, 139 S. Ct. 2369, 2392 (2019) (Alito, J., dissenting).
2. *See, e.g.*, Andrew Jensen Kerr, *The Perfect Opinion*, 12 Wash. U. Jur. Rev. 221, 253–54 (2020).
3. *Korematsu v. United States*, 323 U.S. 214, 247 (1944) (Robert H. Jackson, J., dissenting), *abrogated by Trump v. Hawaii*, 585 U.S. 667 (2018).
4. *Trump v. Hawaii*, 585 U.S. 667, 710 (2018) (Roberts, C. J.).
5. *Delaware v. Pennsylvania*, 598 U.S. 115, 122 (2023) (Jackson, J.).
6. *Id.* at 125.
7. *United States v. Hansen*, 599 U.S. 762, 796 (2023) (Jackson, J., dissenting).
8. *United States v. Sineneng-Smith*, 140 S. Ct. 1575, 1581 (2020) (Ginsburg, J.).
9. *Flowers v. Mississippi*, 139 S. Ct. 2228, 2262 (2019) (Thomas, J., dissenting).
10. Rule B5.2 Block Quotations states, "Quotations of fifty or more words should be single spaced, indented on both sides, justified, and without quotation marks." *The Bluebook: A Uniform System of Citation* (Columbia L. Rev. Ass'n et al., eds., 21st ed. 2020).
11. *Andy Warhol Found. for the Visual Arts, Inc. v. Goldsmith*, 598 U.S. 508, 568 (2023) (Kagan, J., dissenting) (quoting *Emerson v. Davies*, 8 F. Cas. 615, 619 (C.C.D. Mass. 1845)).
12. *Kahler v. Kansas*, 140 S. Ct. 1021, 1043 (2020) (Breyer, J., dissenting).
13. *Kelly v. United States*, 140 S. Ct. 1565, 1574 (2020) (Kagan, J.).

14. *Id.*
15. *Bostock v. Clayton Cnty.*, 590 U.S. 644, 660 (2020) (Gorsuch, J.).
16. *Gamble v. United States*, 139 S. Ct. 1960, 2007 (2019) (Gorsuch, J., dissenting).
17. *Thryv, Inc. v. Click-to-Call Techs., LP*, 590 U.S. 45, 81 (2020) (Gorsuch, J., dissenting).
18. *Ramos v. Louisiana*, 140 S. Ct. 1390, 1426 (2020) (Alito, J., dissenting).
19. *Merck Sharp & Dohme Corp. v. Albrecht*, 139 S. Ct. 1668, 1677 (2019) (Breyer, J.).

CHAPTER 15

1. *Memoirs v. Massachusetts*, 383 U.S. 413, 428 (1966) (Douglas, J., concurring).
2. Kurt Vonnegut, *A Man Without a Country* 23 (Random House 2007).
3. Cecelia Watson, *The Birth of the Semicolon*, Paris Review (Aug. 1, 2019), https://www.theparisreview.org/blog/2019/08/01/the-birth-of-the-semicolon/.
4. *Trump v. Mazars USA, LLP*, 591 U.S. 848, 861–62 (2020) (Roberts, C.J.).
5. *Thole v. U.S. Bank N.A.*, 140 S. Ct. 1615, 1637 (2020) (Sotomayor, J., dissenting).
6. *Lucky Brand Dungarees, Inc. v. Marcel Fashions Grp., Inc.*, 140 S. Ct. 1589, 1594 (2020) (Sotomayor, J.).
7. *Kelly v. United States*, 140 S. Ct. 1565, 1570 (2020) (Kagan, J.).
8. *Ramos v. Louisiana*, 140 S. Ct. 1390, 1394 (2020) (Gorsuch, J.).
9. *June Med. Servs. LLC v. Russo*, 140 S. Ct. 2103, 2113 (2020) (Breyer, J.).
10. *Lac du Flambeau Band of Lake Superior Chippewa Indians v. Coughlin*, 599 U.S. 382, 388 (2023) (Jackson, J.).
11. *Helix Energy Sols. Grp., Inc. v. Hewitt*, 598 U.S. 39, 62 (2023) (Kagan, J.).
12. *Georgia v. Public.Resource.Org, Inc.*, 140 S. Ct. 1498, 1523 (2020) (Ginsburg, J., dissenting).
13. *Salinas v. U.S. R.R. Ret. Bd.*, 592 U.S. 188, 195 (2021) (Sotomayor, J.).
14. *Kisor v. Wilkie*, 139 S. Ct. 2400, 2408 (2019) (Kagan, J.).
15. *Atl. Richfield Co. v. Christian*, 140 S. Ct. 1335, 1363–64 (2020) (Gorsuch, J., concurring and dissenting).
16. *June Med. Servs. LLC*, 140 S. Ct. at 2118 (Breyer, J.).

CHAPTER 16

1. *Philadelphia Newspapers, Inc. v. Hepps*, 475 U.S. 767, 772 (1986).
2. S. Ct. Style G. v (2016).

PART 11

1. Bryan A. Garner, *Interview with Chief Justice G. Roberts, Jr.*, 13 Scribes J. of Leg. Writing 5, 5 (2010).
2. Justice Elena Kagan, *Chief Justice Roberts Receives ALI's Friendly Medal*, C-Span, at 7:18–11:49 (May 23, 2023), https://www.c-span.org/video/?528270-1/justice-kagan-chief-justice-roberts-american-law-institute-award-ceremony.

CHAPTER 17

1. *Biden v. Nebraska*, 600 U.S. 477, 540 (2023) (Kagan, J., dissenting).
2. Letter from Samuel L. Clemons to David Watt Bowser (March 20, 1880), https://www.marktwainproject.org/xtf/view?docId=letters/UCCL01772.xml;style=letter;brand=mtp; John McIntyre, *One-Sentence Wisdom*, Baltimore Sun (March 29, 2015), https://www.baltimoresun.com/opinion/columnists/mcintyre/bal-onesentence-wisdom-20150329-story.html. Twain might be misquoted on adverbs, but the sentiment is similar.
3. James C. Phillips, *The Linguistic Style of Justice Ketanji Brown Jackson*, 127 Penn. State L. Rev. 1, 12–13 (2022). These statistics also include adjectives and adverbs from quoted material. *Id.* at 7.
4. *Kahler v. Kansas*, 140 S. Ct. 1021, 1039 (2020) (Breyer, J., dissenting).
5. *See, e.g., Rimini St., Inc. v. Oracle USA, Inc.*, 139 S. Ct. 873, 878–79 (2019) (Kavanaugh, J.).
6. *See, e.g., Ruan v. United States*, 597 U.S. 450, 470 (2022) (Alito, J., concurring).
7. *See, e.g., Lockhart v. United States*, 577 U.S. 347, 349 (2016) (Sotomayor, J.).
8. *Weyerhaeuser Co. v. FWS*, 139 S. Ct. 361, 368 (2018) (Roberts, C. J.).
9. *Ruan*, 597 U.S. at 450–51 (Breyer, J.).
10. *Rimini St., Inc.*, 139 S. Ct. at 878–79 (Kavanaugh, J.).
11. *Honeycutt v. United States*, 581 U.S. 443, 450 (2017) (Sotomayor, J.).
12. *Edwards v. Vannoy*, 593 U.S. 255, 299 (2021) (Kagan, J., dissenting).
13. *Weyerhaeuser Co.*, 139 S. Ct. at 364–65 (Roberts, C. J.).
14. *Id.*
15. *Taucher v. Brown-Hruska*, 396 F. 3d 1168, 1175 (D.C. Cir. 2005) (Roberts, J.).
16. Univ. of Kentucky, *Chief Justice John Roberts Visits*, YouTube, at 7:18–11:49 (Feb. 2, 2017), https://www.youtube.com/watch?v=2tUAW3dNAwE.

17. *Haaland v. Brackeen*, 599 U.S. 255, 298 (2023) (Gorsuch, J., concurring).
18. *Dubin v. United States*, 599 U.S. 110, 134 (2023) (Gorsuch, J., concurring).
19. *Allen v. Milligan*, 599 U.S. 1, 10 (2023) (Roberts, C. J.)
20. *Abitron Austria GmbH v. Hetronic Int'l, Inc.*, 600 U.S. 412, 445 n.8 (2023) (Sotomayor, J., concurring).
21. *Wilkins v. United States*, 598 U.S. 152, 163–64 (2023) (Sotomayor, J.)
22. Letter from Clemons, *supra* note 2.
23. *Edwards*, 593 U.S. at 300 (Kagan, J., dissenting).

CHAPTER 18

1. *Dobbs v. Jackson Women's Health Org.*, 597 U.S. 215, 354 (2022) (Roberts, C. J., concurring).
2. *Henson v. Santander Consumer USA Inc.*, 582 U.S. 79, 81 (2017) (Gorsuch, J.).
3. Adam Liptak, *#GorsuchStyle Garners a Gusher of Groans*, N.Y. Times, May 1, 2018, at A14d.
4. Ross Guberman, *Judge Gorsuch Is a Gifted Writer*, Legal Writing Pro (Feb. 17. 2017), https://www.legalwritingpro.com/blog/judge-gors uch-gifts/.
5. *See, e.g.*, Nina Varsava, *Elements of Judicial Style: A Quantitative Guide to Neil Gorsuch's Opinion Writing*, 93 NYU L. Rev. Online 75 (2018).
6. *Am. Legion v. Am. Humanist Ass'n*, 139 S. Ct. 2067, 2075 (2019) (Alito, J.) (quoting *In Flanders Fields & Other Poems* 3 (1919)).
7. *Students for Fair Admissions, Inc. v. President & Fellows of Harvard Coll.*, 600 U.S. 181, 307 (2023) (Gorsuch, J., concurring).
8. *Andy Warhol Found. for the Visual Arts, Inc. v. Goldsmith*, 598 U.S. 508, 554 (2023) (Gorsuch, J., concurring).
9. *Arizona v. Navajo Nation*, 599 U.S. 555, 574 (2023) (Gorsuch, J., dissenting).
10. *Jack Daniel's Props, Inc. v. VIP Prods. LLC*, 599 U.S. 140, 153 (2023) (Kagan, J.).
11. *Fornaro v. James*, 416 F.3d 63, 66 (D.C. Cir. 2005).
12. *Health & Hosp. Corp. of Marion Cnty. v. Talevski*, 599 U.S. 166, 232 (2023) (Alito, J., dissenting).
13. Patrick Barry, *The Rule of Three*, 15 JALWD 247, 253–54 (2018).
14. *Biden v. Nebraska*, 600 U.S. 477, 543–44 (2023) (Kagan, J., dissenting).
15. *Students for Fair Admissions, Inc.*, 600 U.S. at 227 (Roberts, C. J.).
16. *Navajo Nation*, 599 U.S. at 575 (Gorsuch, J., dissenting).
17. *Id.* at 574.

18. *Id.* at 577–78.

19. *Id.* at 579.

20. *Andy Warhol Found. for the Visual Arts, Inc.*, 598 U.S. at 593 (Kagan, J., dissenting).

21. *Students for Fair Admissions, Inc.*, 600 U.S. at 230 (Roberts, C. J.).

22. *Andy Warhol Found. for the Visual Arts, Inc.*, 598 U.S. at 584 (Kagan, J., dissenting).

23. *Torres v. Madrid*, 592 U.S. 306, 323 (2021) (Roberts, C. J.).

24. *Id.* at 344 (Gorsuch, J., dissenting).

25. *Ysleta Del Sur Pueblo v. Texas*, 142 S. Ct. 1929, 1947 (2022) (Roberts, C. J., dissenting).

26. *Navajo Nation*, 599 U.S. at 599 (Gorsuch, J., dissenting).

27. *Jones v. Hendrix*, 599 U.S. 465, 530 (2023) (Jackson, J., dissenting).

28. *Students for Fair Admissions, Inc.*, 600 U.S. at 205 (Roberts, C. J.).

29. *Id.* at 397 (Jackson, J., dissenting).

CHAPTER 19

1. *Niz-Chavez v. Garland*, 593 U.S. 155, 172 (2021).

2. *Bostock v. Clayton Cnty.*, 590 U.S. 644, 662 (2020) (Gorsuch, J.).

3. *See, e.g.,* "Since." Merriam-Webster.com, https://www.merriam-webster.com/dictionary/since.

4. "Because." Merriam-Webster.com, https://www.merriam-webster.com/dictionary/because.

5. For example, Justice Kavanaugh asked, "can you just go to the second question **since** time's limited?" Oral Argument at 59:52, *Harry Schein, Inc. v. Archer & White Sales, Inc.*, 139 S. Ct. 524 (2019), https://www.oyez.org/cases/2020/19-963.

6. Chief Justice Roberts, along with Justices Thomas, Breyer, Alito, and Jackson, have used *since* to mean *because*. Gorsuch's and Sotomayor's single references, assuming they were intentional instead of mistakes, tilt the scale here to 5–4. *Liu v. SEC*, 140 S. Ct. 1936, 1948 (2020) (Sotomayor, J.) ("There, the Court found that the additional statutory language must be given effect **since** the section 'does not, after all, authorize . . . "equitable relief" at large.'"); *NCAA v. Alston*, 141 S. Ct. 2141, 2162 (2021) (Gorsuch, J.) ("'To be sure, these two questions can be collapsed into one,'" **since** a "'legitimate objective that is not promoted by the challenged restraint can be equally served by simply abandoning the restraint, which is surely a less restrictive alternative.'").

7. *Uzuegbunam v. Preczewski*, 592 U.S. 279, 304 (2021) (Roberts, C. J., dissenting).

8. *Trump v. Mazars USA, LLP*, 591 U.S. 848, 859 (2020) (Roberts, C. J.).

9. *Nieves v. Bartlett*, 139 S. Ct. 1715, 1725 n.1 (2019) (Roberts, C. J.).

10. *Am. Legion v. Am. Humanist Ass'n*, 139 S. Ct. 2067, 2108 (2019) (Ginsburg, J., dissenting).

11. *See, e.g.*, Josh Weinberger, *Words Matter*, Wix (Jan. 19, 2021), https://www.wix.com/wordsmatter/blog/2021/01/can-you-start-a-sentence-with-because/#:~:text=The%20rule%20is%20that%20you,up%20with%20a%20fragmented%20sentence.

12. *Atl. Richfield Co. v. Christian*, 140 S. Ct. 1335, 1361 (2020) (Alito, J., concurring).

13. *DHS v. Thuraissigiam*, 140 S. Ct. 1959, 1982 (2020) (Alito, J.).

14. *Id.*

15. *Barton v. Barr*, 140 S. Ct. 1442, 1454 (2020) (Sotomayor, J., dissenting).

16. *Brnovich v. DNC*, 141 S. Ct. 2321, 2350–51 (2021) (Kagan, J., dissenting).

CHAPTER 20

1. *Ford Motor Co. v. Mont. Eighth Jud. Dist. Ct.*, 141 S. Ct. 1017, 1034 (2021) (Gorsuch, J., concurring).

2. A. E. Hotchner, *Papa Hemingway* 69 (1966).

3. Conor Friedersdorf, *Why Clarence Thomas Uses Simple Words in His Opinions*, Atlantic (Feb. 20, 2013), https://www.theatlantic.com/national/archive/2013/02/why-clarence-thomas-uses-simple-words-in-his-opinions/273326/.

4. *Id.*

5. *Kahler v. Kansas*, 140 S. Ct. 1021, 1037 (2020) (Kagan, J.).

6. *Lomax v. Ortiz-Marquez*, 140 S. Ct. 1721, 1725 (2020) (Kagan, J.).

7. *Kahler*, 140 S. Ct. at 1031 (Kagan, J.).

8. *Allen v. Cooper*, 589 U.S. 248, 255 (2020) (Kagan, J.).

9. *Sturgeon v. Frost*, 587 U.S. 28, 35 (2019) (Kagan, J.).

10. *Sanchez v. Mayorkas*, 593 U.S. 409, 417 (2021) (Kagan, J.).

11. George Dorrill, *"Don't Begin Sentences with But" Is a Writing Myth*, 24 Quarterly 23 (Fall 2002).

12. Anand Giridharadas, *Follow My Logic?*, N.Y. Times, May 30, 2010, at WK3.

13. *Henson v. Santander Cons. USA Inc.*, 582 U.S. 79, 81 (2017) (Gorsuch, J.).

14. *Henry Schein Inc. v. Archer & White Sales, Inc.*, 139 S. Ct. 524, 530 (2019) (Kavanaugh, J.).

15. *FWS v. Sierra Club, Inc.*, 592 U.S. 261, 265 (2021) (Barrett, J.).

16. *See* Jill Barton, *Supreme Court Splits—On Grammar and Writing Style*, 17 Scribes J. Legal Writing 33 (2016–17).

17. Unpublished interim order: *United States v. Texas*, 1:21-cv-00796-RP (W.D. Tex. Oct. 6, 2021).

18. Note that *so* also can be used as an intensifier and in phrases such as "to do so," and "so-called rule." In total, *so* was used 5,246 in five years (including in quotes).

CHAPTER 21

1. *Washington v. W.C. Dawson & Co.*, 264 U.S. 219, 236 (1924) (Brandeis, J., dissenting).

2. *Jack Daniel's Props, Inc. v. VIP Prods. LLC*, 599 U.S. 140, 148 (2023) (Kagan, J.).

3. *Yellen v. Confederated Tribes of Chehalis Rsrv.*, 141 S. Ct. 2434 (2021); *Facebook, Inc. v. Duguid*, 592 U.S. 395 (2021); *Lockhart v. United States*, 577 U.S. 347 (2016).

4. *Facebook, Inc.*, 592 U.S. at 413 (Alito, J., concurring).

5. *Confederated Tribes of Chehalis Rsrv.*, 141 S. Ct. at 2454 (Gorsuch, J., dissenting).

6. *Oklahoma v. Castro-Huerta*, 597 U.S. 629, 674 n.4 (2022) (Gorsuch, J., dissenting).

7. *Cameron v. EMW Women's Surgical Ctr., P.S.C.*, 595 U.S. 267, 294 (2022) (Sotomayor, J., dissenting).

8. *Carson v. Makin*, 596 U.S. 767, 810 (2022) (Sotomayor, J., dissenting).

9. *Reed v. Texas*, 140 S. Ct. 686, 687 (2020) (Sotomayor, J.) (denial of cert).

10. Apologies to Chief Justice Roberts for this alteration. See the well-written and grammatically correct *Weyerhaeuser Co. v. FWS*, 139 S. Ct. 361 (2018) (Roberts, C.J.).

11. *Dep't of Com. v. New York*, 139 S. Ct. 2551, 2583 (2019) (Thomas, J., concurring in part and dissenting in part).

12. *Seila Law LLC v. CFPB*, 140 S. Ct. 2183, 2238 (2020) (Kagan, J., concurring in judgment and dissenting in part).

13. *Chicago v. Fulton*, 592 U.S. 154, 158 (2021) (Alito, J.).

14. *Torres v. Madrid*, 592 U.S. 306, 350 (2021) (Gorsuch, J., dissenting).

15. *Manhattan Cmty. Access Corp. v. Halleck*, 139 S. Ct. 1921, 1934 (2019) (Kavanaugh, J.).

16. *Florida v. Georgia*, 592 U.S. 433, 443 (2021) (Barrett, J.).

17. *Dutra Grp. v. Batterton*, 588 U.S. 358, 382 (2019) (Ginsburg, J., dissenting).

18. Most justices dangle rarely. In nearly 1,000 pages of his written opinions, Roberts only dangled a modifier a few times. *See, e.g., Dobbs v. Jackson Women's Health Org.*, 597 U.S. 215, 351 (2022) (Roberts, C. J., concurring) (**Assuming** that prevention of fetal pain is a legitimate state interest after *Gonzales*, **there seems** to be no reason why viability would be relevant to the permissibility of such laws.).

19. *Tenn. Wine & Spirits Retailers Ass'n v. Thomas*, 139 S. Ct. 2449, 2483 (2019) (Gorsuch, J., dissenting).

20. *Lockhart*, 577 U.S. at 362 (Kagan, J., dissenting).

21. 47 U.S.C. § 227(a)(1); *Facebook, Inc.*, 592 U.S. at 402 (Sotomayor, J.).

22. *Becerra v. Empire Health Found.*, 597 U.S. 424, 430 (2022) (Kagan, J.) ("With that under your belt, you might be ready to absorb the relevant statutory language (**but don't bet on it**).").

23. *Facebook, Inc.*, 592 U.S. at 404 (Sotomayor, J.).

24. *Id.* at 403.

25. *Id.* at 411 (Alito, J., concurring).

26. *Id.*

27. *Id.*

28. *Id.*

29. *Id.* at 412.

30. *See id.*

31. *Lockhart*, 577 U.S. at 362 (Kagan, J., dissenting).

32. *Id.* at 357 (Sotomayor, J.).

33. Oral Argument at 1:03:07, *Facebook, Inc. v. Duguid*, 592 U.S. 395 (2021) (Kagan, J.), https://www.oyez.org/cases/2020/19-511.

CHAPTER 22

1. Justice Brett Kavanaugh, Notre Dame L. Rev. Symp. (Jan. 26, 2023), at 21:35, https://www.youtube.com/watch?v=b8w9xttTLwc&t=3s.

2. *United States v. Farmer*, 583 F.3d 131, 135 (2d Cir. 2009).

3. Brief for Defendant-Appellant, *United States v. Farmer*, 583 F.3d 131 (2d Cir. 2009) (No. 07-2729) 2008 WL 7898526 at *30.

4. Stav Atir and Melissa J. Ferguson, *How Gender Determines the Way We Speak about Professionals*, 115 Proceedings Nat'l Acad. of Sciences 28, 7278 (June 25, 2018).

5. *Id.*

6. *See United States v. Virginia*, 518 U.S. 515, 532 (1996) (Ginsburg, J.).

7. *See id.* at 534.

8. *Wilkins v. United States*, 598 U.S. 152, 155 (2023) (Sotomayor, J.).

9. *Bartenwerfer v. Buckley*, 598 U.S. 69, 82 (2023) (Barrett, J.).

10. *Id.* at 72.

11. *Id.* at 74.

12. *Id.* at 75.

13. *Cummings v. Premier Rehab Keller, P.L.L.C.*, 596 U.S. 212, 216–17 (2022) (Roberts, C.J.).

14. *FWS v. Sierra Club, Inc.*, 592 U.S. 261, 264 (2021) (Barrett, J.).

15. *DHS v. Regents of Univ. of Cal.*, 140 S. Ct. 1891, 1901 (2020) (Roberts, C.J.).

16. Scott Sayare, *French Bid Farewell to 'Mademoiselle,'* N.Y. Times, Feb. 22, 2012, at A5.

17. *Id.*

18. *See, e.g., Loving v. Virginia*, 388 U.S. 1, 5 (1967) (Warren, J.) (using "Mrs." Loving); *Mapp v. Ohio*, 367 U.S. 643, 644 (1961) (Clark, J.) (using "Miss" Mapp); *but see, e.g., House v. Bell*, 547 U.S. 518, 562 (2006) (Roberts, C.J., concurring and dissenting) (using "Ms." Parker and "Ms." Letner).

19. *Am. Legion v. Am. Humanist Ass'n*, 139 S. Ct. 2067, 2077 (2019) (Alito, J.).

20. *Carson v. Makin*, 596 U.S. 767, 775 (2022) (Roberts, C.J.).

21. *Uzuegbunam v. Preczewski*, 592 U.S 279, 294 (2021) (Roberts, C. J., dissenting).

22. *Knick v. Twp. of Scott*, 588 U.S. 180, 185 (2019) (Roberts, C.J.).

23. "Mx.: A gender-neutral title of courtesy prefixed to a person's surname . . . ." Oxford English Dictionary, https://www.oed.com/view/Entry/37988089?rskey=nIE7Dx&result=2#eid.

24. Words We're Watching, Merriam-Webster.com, https://www.merriam-webster.com/words-at-play/mx-gender-neutral-title.

25. *Harmon v. Lewandowski*, No. 220CV09437MEMFMRWX, 2022 WL 1161142, at *1 n.2 (C.D. Cal. Mar. 31, 2022).

26. *Doe v. Pa. Dep't of Corr.*, No. 120CV00023SPBRAL, 2021 WL 1583556, at *13 (W.D. Pa. Feb. 19, 2021).

27. Justice Alito has done so once in five years, but was referring to counsel. *Facebook, Inc. v. Duguid*, 592 U.S. 395, 410 (2021) (Alito, J., concurring) (Even grammar, according to **Mr.** Garner, is ordinarily just "an attempt to describe the English language as it is actually used.").

28. *Brown v. Davenport*, 596 U.S. 118, 122 (2022) (Gorsuch, J.).

29. *Bostock v. Clayton Cnty.*, 590 U.S. 644, 653–54 (2020) (Gorsuch, J.).

30. *Kelly v. United States*, 140 S. Ct. 1565, 1569 (2020) (Kagan, J.).

31. *Bucklew v. Precythe*, 139 S. Ct. 1112, 1121–22 (2019) (Gorsuch, J.).

32. *Seila Law LLC v. CFPB*, 140 S. Ct. 2183, 2192 (2020) (Roberts, C.J.).

33. *Regents of Univ. of Cal.*, 140 S. Ct. at 1904 (Roberts, C. J.).
34. *Turkiye Halk Bankasi A. S. v. United States*, 598 U.S. 264, 272 (2023) (Kavanaugh, J.).
35. *New York v. New Jersey*, 598 U.S. 218, 221 (2023) (Kavanaugh, J.).
36. *Axon Enterprise, Inc. v. FTC*, 598 U.S. 175, 199 (2023) (Thomas, J., concurring).
37. *Seila Law LLC*, 140 S. Ct. at 2214 (Thomas, J., concurring in part and dissenting in part).
38. *Agency for Int'l Dev. v. All. for Open Soc'y Int'l, Inc.*, 140 S. Ct. 2082, 2085 (2020) (Kavanaugh, J.).
39. *Barr v. Am. Ass'n of Pol. Consultants, Inc.*, 140 S. Ct. 2335, 2344 (2020) (Kavanaugh, J.).
40. *New York*, 598 U.S. at 221 (Kavanaugh, J.).
41. *United States v. Vaello Madero*, 596 U.S. 159, 166 (2022) (Kavanaugh, J.).
42. *Turkiye Halk Bankasi A. S.*, 598 U.S. at 279 (Kavanaugh, J.).
43. *Arellano v. McDonough*, 598 U.S. 1, 7 (2023) (Barrett, J.).
44. *Trump v. Vance*, 591 U.S. 786, 794–95 (2020) (Roberts, C. J.).
45. *Uzuegbunam*, 592 U.S. at 304 (Roberts, C. J., dissenting).
46. *Am. Ass'n of Pol. Consultants, Inc.*, 140 S. Ct. at 2344 (Kavanaugh, J.); *Regents of Univ. of Cal.*, 140 S. Ct. at 1932 (Kavanaugh, J., concurring).
47. *Regents of Univ. of Cal.*, 140 S. Ct. at 1918 (Thomas, J., concurring).
48. *Vaello Madero*, 596 U.S. at 173 (Thomas, J., concurring).
49. *Terry v. United States*, 593 U.S. 486, 491 (2021) (Thomas, J.).
50. *Edwards v. Vannoy*, 593 U.S. 255, 289 (2021) (Gorsuch, J., concurring).

CHAPTER 23

1. *Kimble v. Marvel Ent., LLC*, 576 U.S. 446, 465 (2015).
2. *Hemingway's 4 Rules for Writing Well*, Int'l Ass'n of Bus. Communicators Chicago (Dec. 21, 2011), http://chicago.iabc.com/2011/12/hemingw ays-4-rules-for-writing-well/.
3. *Felkner v. Jackson*, 562 U.S. 594, 598 (2011) (Roberts, C. J).
4. *McGirt v. Oklahoma*, 140 S. Ct. 2452, 2460 (2020) (Gorsuch, J.).
5. *United States v. Haymond*, 139 S. Ct. 2369, 2389 (2019) (Alito, J., dissenting).
6. *Federal Republic of Ger. v. Philipp*, 592 U.S. 169, 175 (2021) (Roberts, C. J.).
7. *Facebook, Inc. v. Duguid*, 592 U.S. 395, 413 (2021) (Alito, J., concurring).
8. *DHS v. Thuraissigiam*, 140 S. Ct. 1959, 2000 (2020) (Sotomayor, J., dissenting).

9. *DHS v. Regents of Univ. of Cal.*, 140 S. Ct. 1891, 1916 (2020) (Roberts, C. J.).
10. *Uzuegbunam v. Preczewski*, 592 U.S. 279, 290 (2021) (Thomas, J.).
11. *Google LLC v. Oracle Am., Inc.*, 141 S. Ct. 1183, 1211 (2021) (Thomas, J., dissenting).
12. *Espinoza v. Mont. Dep't of Rev.*, 140 S. Ct. 2246, 2263 (2020) (Roberts, C. J.) (emphasis added).
13. *Nielsen v. Preap*, 139 S. Ct. 954, 962 (2019) (Alito, J.).
14. *Allen v. Cooper*, 589 U.S. 248, 255 (2020) (Kagan, J.).
15. *Borden v. United States*, 593 U.S. 420, 441 (2021) (Kagan, J.).
16. *Little Sisters Poor Saints Peter & Paul Home v. Pennsylvania.*, 140 S. Ct. 2367, 2395 (2020) (Alito, J., concurring).

CHAPTER 24

1. *Rucho v. Common Cause*, 139 S. Ct. 2484, 2518 (2019) (Kagan, J., dissenting).
2. *Flowers v. Mississippi*, 139 S. Ct. 2228, 2262 (2019) (Thomas, J., dissenting).
3. *June Med. Servs. LLC v. Russo*, 140 S. Ct. 2103, 2119 (2020) (Breyer, J.).
4. *See* S. Ct. Style G. § 10.11(d) (2016).
5. *Carney v. Adams*, 592 U.S. 53, 56 (2020) (Breyer, J.).
6. *Sturgeon v. Frost*, 587 U.S. 28, 57 (2019) (Kagan, J.).
7. *United States v. Davis*, 139 S. Ct. 2319, 2337 (2019) (Kavanaugh, J., dissenting).
8. *Holguin-Hernandez v. United States*, 140 S. Ct. 762, 764 (2020) (Breyer, J.).
9. *Chicago v. Fulton*, 592 U.S. 154, 163 (Sotomayor, J., concurring).
10. *Atl. Richfield Co. v. Christian*, 140 S. Ct. 1335, 1362 (2020) (Gorsuch, J., concurring and dissenting).
11. *Id.* at 1348 (Roberts, C. J.).
12. *Stokeling v. United States*, 139 S. Ct. 544, 558 (2019) (Sotomayor, J., dissenting).
13. *Azar v. Allina Health Services*, 139 S. Ct. 1804, 1809 (2019) (Gorsuch, J.).
14. *Bucklew v. Precythe*, 139 S. Ct. 1112, 1134 n.5 (2019) (Gorsuch, J.).
15. *Kahler v. Kansas*, 140 S. Ct. 1021, 1046 (2020) (Breyer, J., dissenting).
16. *Kelly v. United States*, 140 S. Ct. 1565, 1569 (2020) (Kagan, J.).
17. *Trump v. Mazars USA, LLP*, 591 U.S. 848, 853 (2020) (Roberts, C. J.).
18. *Allen v. Milligan*, 599 U.S. 1, 36 (2023) (Roberts, C. J.).
19. *Borden v. United States*, 593 U.S. 420, 440 n.8 (2021) (Kagan, J.).
20. *Seila Law LLC v. CFPB*, 140 S. Ct. 2183, 2233 (2020) (Kagan, J., concurring in judgment and dissenting in part).

CHAPTER 25

1. *NLRB v. Federbush Co.,* 121 F.2d 954, 957 (2d Cir. 1941).
2. *Bostock v. Clayton Cnty.,* 590 U.S. 644, 677 (2020) (Gorsuch, J.).
3. *Georgia v. Public.Resource.Org, Inc..,* 140 S. Ct. 1498, 1513 (2020) (Roberts, C. J.).
4. *Rucho v. Common Cause,* 139 S. Ct. 2484, 2521 (2019) (Kagan, J., dissenting).
5. *New Prime Inc. v. Oliveira,* 139 S. Ct. 532, 542 (2019) (Gorsuch, J.).
6. *Va. Uranium, Inc. v. Warren,* 139 S. Ct. 1894, 1919 (2019) (Roberts, C. J., dissenting).
7. *Kahler v. Kansas,* 140 S. Ct. 1021, 1026 (2020) (Kagan, J.).
8. *Gundy v. United States,* 139 S. Ct. 2116, 2128 (2019) (Kagan, J.).
9. *Pereida v. Wilkinson,* 592 U.S. 224, 228–29 (2021) (Gorsuch, J.).
10. *Allen v. Cooper,* 589 U.S. 248, 252 (2020) (Kagan, J.).

CHAPTER 26

1. *Planned Parenthood of Se. Pa. v. Casey,* 505 U.S. 833, 851 (1992).
2. John Fowles, *The French Lieutenant's Woman* 72 (1969).
3. Heidi K. Brown, *Get with the Pronoun,* 17 JALWD 61, 63 (2020) ("While law often (understandably) takes time to catch up to societal change, as legal writers, we should actively ramp up our awareness about the growing use and acceptance of non-binary language across many facets of our American society.").
4. Previously, the Court generally avoided pronouns when referring to transgender individuals, with a few exceptions. *See, e.g., Farmer v. Brennan,* 511 U.S. 825, 851 (1994) (Souter, J.) ("[T]he Deputy Solicitor General . . . suggested that affirmance was nevertheless proper because 'there is no present threat' that petitioner will be placed in a setting where **he** would face a 'continuing threat of physical injury . . . .'").
5. *Bostock v. Clayton Cnty.,* 590 U.S. 644, 653–54 (2020) (Gorsuch, J.).
6. *Id.* at 731–32 (Alito, J., dissenting).
7. *See id.;* Brief for Petitioner, *Bostock v. Clayton Cnty.,* 590 U.S. 644 (2020), 2019 WL 3958416, at *8 n.3.
8. *See, e.g.,* Brief for Respondent, *Santos-Zacaria v. Garland,* 598 U.S. 411 (2023), 2022 WL 17885060, at *6–7 ("Petitioner is a transgender woman and a native and citizen of Guatemala. **She** left Guatemala for Mexico in **her** early teens, and **she** first unlawfully entered the United States in 2008.").

9. *Santos-Zacaria v. Garland*, 598 U.S. 411, 414 (2023) (Jackson, J.).

10. *Id.* at 431 (Alito, J., concurring).

11. *See, e.g.*, *Greer v. United States*, 593 U.S. 503, 508 (2021) (Kavanaugh, J.) ("If a **person** is a **felon**, **he** ordinarily knows **he** is a felon."); *Caniglia v. Strom*, 593 U.S. 194, 207 (2021) (Kavanaugh, J., concurring) ("Suppose that a **woman** calls a healthcare hotline or 911 and says that **she** is contemplating suicide, that **she** has firearms in her home, and that **she** might as well die."); *Bartenwerfer v. Buckley*, 598 U.S. 69, 82 (2023) (Barrett, J.) ("For instance, though an **employer** is generally accountable for the wrongdoing of an employee, **he** usually can escape liability if **he** proves that the employee's action was committed outside the scope of employment."). In five years, Justice Thomas did not use *she* generically, but he also did not use *he or she* outside of quotes, indicating he likely writes around the issue.

12. *Yellen v. Confederated Tribes of Chehalis Rsrv.*, 141 S. Ct. 2434, 2448 (2021) (Sotomayor, J.).

13. *Google LLC v. Oracle Am., Inc.*, 141 S. Ct. 1183, 1193 (2021) (Breyer, J.).

14. *Biestek v. Berryhill*, 139 S. Ct. 1148, 1154 (2019) (Kagan, J.).

15. *TransUnion LLC v. Ramirez*, 594 U.S. 413, 427 (2021) (Kavanaugh, J.).

16. *Nestle USA, Inc. v. Doe*, 593 U.S. 628, 638 (2021) (Thomas, J.).

17. *Fulton v. Philadelphia*, 593 U.S. 522, 613 (2021) (Alito, J., concurring).

18. *See, e.g.*, Farhad Manjoo, *It's Time for 'They,'* N.Y. Times, July 10, 2019, at Opinion.

19. *AMG Capital Mgmt., LLC v. FTC*, 593 U.S. 67, 70 (2021) (Breyer, J.).

20. *Ohio Adjutant Gen.'s Dep't v. FLRA*, 598 U.S. 449, 467 (2023) (Alito, J., dissenting).

21. *Ramos v. Louisiana*, 140 S. Ct. 1390, 1408 (2020) (Gorsuch, J.).

22. *Dyjak v. Wilkerson*, No. 21-2012, 2022 WL 1285221, at *1 n.1 (7th Cir. Apr. 29, 2022).

23. *See, e.g.*, Brown, *supra* note 3.

24. One exception, likely a mistaken use of the singular *they*, predates my 2018–2023 study: *Lockhart v. United States*, 577 U.S. 347, 357 (2016) (Sotomayor, J.) ("[This] list is hardly the way an average person, or even an average lawyer, would set about to describe the relevant conduct if **they** had started from scratch.").

25. Oral Argument at 5:25, *Kennedy v. Bremerton Sch. Dist.*, 597 U.S. 507 (2022) (Sotomayor, J.), https://www.oyez.org/cases/2021/21-418.

26. Oral Argument at 8:22, *Polselli v. IRS*, 598 U.S. 432 (2023) (Kagan, J.), https://www.oyez.org/cases/2022/21-1599.

27. Oral Argument at 1:23:23 *Groff v. Dejoy*, 600 U.S. 447 (2023) (Alito, J.), https://www.oyez.org/cases/2022/22-174.

28. *BP P.L.C. v. Mayor & City Council of Baltimore*, 593 U.S. 230, 252 (2021) (Sotomayor, J., dissenting).

29. *Id.*

30. *Houston Cmty. College Sys. v. Wilson*, 595 U.S. 468, 482 (2022) (Gorsuch, J.).

31. *Am. Legion v. Am. Humanist Ass'n*, 139 S. Ct. 2067, 2076 (2019) (Alito, J.).

32. *Id.* at 2101 (Gorsuch, J., concurring).

33. *Amgen Inc. v. Sanofi*, 598 U.S. 594, 613 (2023) (Gorsuch, J.).

34. *See, e.g.*, Tyler Kepner, *The Rays Are Better Than Everyone*, N.Y. Times, May 5, 2023, at B10. ("The Rays, as usual, are getting a lot for their money: **Their** player payroll ranks among the majors' lowest . . . but **they** have dominated . . . .").

35. One *they* reference could be read to have either *players* or *team* as the antecedent. *Kennedy v. Bremerton Sch. Dist.*, 597 U.S. 507, 562 (2022) (Sotomayor, J., dissenting) ("Kennedy told the District that he began his prayers alone and that **players** followed each other over time until a majority of the team joined him, an evolution showing coercive pressure at work. Kennedy does not defend his longstanding practice of leading the **team** in prayer out loud on the field as **they** kneeled around him.").

36. Oral Argument at 1:21:21, *Kennedy v. Bremerton Sch. Dist.*, 597 U.S. 507 (2022) (Alito, J.), https://www.oyez.org/cases/2021/21-418.

37. Oral Argument at 4:41, *Cruz v. Arizona*, 598 U.S. 17 (2023) (Roberts, C. J.), https://www.oyez.org/cases/2022/21-846.

38. Oral Argument at 43:49, *Groff v. Dejoy*, 600 U.S. 447 (2023) (Jackson, J.), https://www.oyez.org/cases/2022/22-174.

39. Oral Argument at 31:42, *Polselli v. IRS*, 598 U.S. 432 (2023) (Kagan, J.), https://www.oyez.org/cases/2022/21-1599.

40. *California v. Texas*, 593 U.S. 659, 712 (2021) (Alito, J., dissenting); *cf. West Virginia v. EPA*, 597 U.S. 697, 724 (2022) (Roberts, C. J.) ("And the Agency's discovery allowed it to adopt a regulatory program that Congress had conspicuously and repeatedly declined to enact **itself**.").

41. *United States v. Arthrex, Inc.*, 594 U.S. 1, 12 (2021) (Roberts, C. J.) (quoting Art. II, § 2, cl. 2.)

42. *Carr v. Saul*, 593 U.S. 83, 96 (2021).

43. *Collins v. Yellen*, 141 S. Ct. 1761, 1770 (2021) (Alito, J.).

44. *Id.* at 1771.

45. *Id.* at 1796 (Gorsuch, J., concurring).

46. *Id.* at 1797.

47. *Dobbs v. Jackson Women's Health Org.*, 597 U.S. 215, 380 (2022) (Breyer, Sotomayor, and Kagan, JJ., dissenting).

48. *Badgerow v. Walters*, 596 U.S. 1, 31 (2022) (Breyer, J., dissenting).

49. *Cedar Point Nursery v. Hassid*, 594 U.S. 139, 144 (2021) (Roberts, C. J.).

50. *Axon Enter., Inc. v. FTC*, 598 U.S. 175, 206 (2023) (Gorsuch, J. concurring).

51. *MOAC Mall Holdings LLC v. Transform Holdco LLC*, 598 U.S. 288, 299 (2023) (Jackson, J.).

52. *Ysleta Del Sur Pueblo v. Texas*, 596 U.S. 685, 716 (2022) (Roberts, C. J., dissenting).

53. *Cedar Point Nursery*, 594 U.S. at 167 (Breyer, J., dissenting).

54. *Reed v. Goertz*, 598 U.S. 230, 250 n.5 (2023) (Thomas, J., dissenting).

55. *Cruz v. Arizona*, 598 U.S. 17, 27 (2023) (Sotomayor, J.).

56. *Andy Warhol Found. for the Visual Arts, Inc. v. Goldsmith*, 598 U.S. 508, 535 (2023) (Sotomayor, J.)

57. *Ohio Adjutant Gen.'s Dep't*, 598 U.S. at 465 (Alito, J., dissenting).

58. *Andrus v. Texas*, 142 S. Ct. 1866, 1870 (2022) (Sotomayor, J., dissenting) (denial of cert).

59. *Sonia Sotomayor Freedom to Write Lecture*, C-Span, at 1:04:08 (May 5, 2013), https://www.c-span.org/video/?312669-1/sonia-sotomayor-freedom-write-lecture.

60. *Id.* at 28:00.

CHAPTER 27

1. *Lange v. California*, 141 S. Ct. 2011, 2033 (2021) (Roberts, C. J., concurring).

2. *See, e.g.*, Benjamin Dreyer, *Dreyer's Guide to English* 3 (2019).

3. *Weyerhaeuser Co. v. FWS*, 139 S. Ct. 361, 365 (2018) (Roberts, C. J.).

4. *Fulton v. Philadelphia*, 593 U.S. 522, 624 (2021) (Gorsuch, J., concurring).

5. *HollyFrontier Cheyenne Refining, LLC v. Renewable Fuels Ass'n*, 141 S. Ct. 2172, 2180 (2021) (Gorsuch, J.).

6. *Garland v. Ming Dai*, 593 U.S. 357, 371 (2021) (Gorsuch, J.).

7. *Thryv, Inc. v. Click-To-Call Techs., LP*, 590 U.S. 45, 69 (2020) (Gorsuch, J., dissenting).

8. *Torres v. Madrid*, 592 U.S. 306, 329 (2021) (Gorsuch, J., dissenting).

9. *Id.* at 332.

10. *Id.* at 334.

11. *Dreyer's Guide to English* at 161.

12. *Id.*

13. *RNC v. DNC*, 140 S. Ct. 1205, 1210 (2020) (Ginsburg, J., dissenting).

14. *Haaland v. Brackeen*, 599 U.S. 255, 327 (2023) (Gorsuch, J., concurring).

15. *Bostock v. Clayton Cty.*, 590 U.S. 644, 787 (2020) (Kavanaugh, J., dissenting).

16. *Biden v. Nebraska*, 600 U.S. 477, 512 (2023) (Barrett, J., concurring).

CHAPTER 28

1. *United States v. Nickerson*, 58 U.S. 204, 209 (1854).

2. *Espinoza v. Mont. Dep't of Rev.*, 140 S. Ct. 2246, 2254 (2020) (Roberts, C. J.).

3. *Nat'l Pork Producers Council v. Ross*, 598 U.S. 356, 404 (2023) (Kavanaugh, J., concurring and dissenting).

4. *Madison v. Alabama*, 139 S. Ct. 718, 727 (2019) (Kagan, J.).

5. *Herrera v. Wyoming*, 139 S. Ct. 1686, 1693 (2019) (Sotomayor, J.).

6. *Madison*, 139 S. Ct. at 727 (Kagan, J.).

7. *Sturgeon v. Frost*, 587 U.S. 28, 57 (2019) (Kagan, J.).

8. *Van Buren v. United States*, 141 S. Ct. 1648, 1653 (2021) (Barrett, J.).

9. *Chiafalo v. Washington*, 591 U.S. 578, 583 (2020) (Kagan, J.).

10. *Id.* at 585.

11. *Id.* at 592.

CHAPTER 29

1. *Biden v. Texas*, 597 U.S. 785, 798 (2022).

2. *See* Lucius Adelno Sherman, *Analytics of Literature* 259 (1893).

3. William Shakespeare, *Hamlet*, Act III, Scene 1, lines 55–56 (1601); *Merchant of Venice*, Act II, Scene 7, line 65 (1605); *Richard III*, Act 5, Scene 4, line 6 (1591).

4. James C. Phillips, *The Linguistic Style of Justice Ketanji Brown Jackson*, 127 Penn. State L. Rev. 1, 10 (2022).

5. *Id.* at 11.

6. *Samia v. United States*, 599 U.S. 635, 657–58 (2023) (Kagan, J., dissenting).

7. Harvard Law, *A Conversation with U.S. Supreme Court Justice Elena Kagan*, YouTube, at 20:40 (Sept. 14, 2017), https://www.youtube.com/watch?v=ZmCTqtrMMXk.

8. *United States v. Windsor*, 570 U.S. 744, 799 (2013) (Scalia, J., dissenting).

9. *Sykes v. United States*, 564 U.S. 1, 30 (2011) (Scalia, J., dissenting).

10. *Atl. Richfield Co. v. Christian*, 140 S. Ct. 1335, 1346 (2020) (Roberts, C. J.).

11. *Students for Fair Admissions, Inc. v. President & Fellows of Harvard Coll.*, 600 U.S. 181 (2023).

12. *Id.* at 204, 217 (Roberts, C. J.).
13. *Id.* at 268 (Thomas, J., concurring).
14. *Id.* at 363 (Sotomayor, J., dissenting).
15. *Id.* at 296 (Gorsuch, J., concurring).
16. *Id.* at 316 (Kavanaugh, J., concurring).
17. *Id.* at 393 (Jackson, J., dissenting).

CHAPTER 30

1. *Boechler, P.C. v. Commissioner*, 596 U.S. 199, 205 (2022).
2. *See, e.g.*, William Strunk Jr. and E. B. White, *The Elements of Style* 58 (4th ed. 2000) ("[T]he construction should be avoided unless the writer wishes to place additional stress on the adverb.").
3. Gertrude Block, *The Awkward 'For' in 'For Free'*, 36 Pa. Law. 58 (May/June 2014).
4. *Madison v. Alabama*, 139 S. Ct. 718, 726–27 (2019) (Kagan, J.).
5. *Banister v. Davis*, 140 S. Ct. 1698, 1709 (2020) (Kagan, J.).
6. *Google LLC v. Oracle Am., Inc.*, 141 S. Ct. 1183, 1211 (2021) (Thomas, J., dissenting).
7. *Fort Bend Cnty. v. Davis*, 139 S. Ct. 1843, 1851–52 (2019) (Ginsburg, J.).
8. *FWS v. Sierra Club, Inc.*, 592 U.S. 261, 268 (2021) (Barrett, J.).
9. *Lamps Plus, Inc. v. Varela*, 139 S. Ct. 1407, 1425 (2019) (Breyer, J., dissenting).
10. *Gamble v. United States*, 139 S. Ct. 1960, 1990 (2019) (Ginsburg, J., dissenting).

CHAPTER 31

1. *Orloff v. Willoughby*, 345 U.S. 83, 87 (1953).
2. *Jones v. Mississippi*, 593 U.S. 98, 151 (2021) (Sotomayor, J., dissenting).
3. *Lac du Flambeau Band of Lake Superior Chippewa Indians v. Coughlin*, 599 U.S. 382, 413 (2023) (Gorsuch, J., dissenting).
4. *Andy Warhol Found. for the Visual Arts, Inc. v. Goldsmith*, 598 U.S. 508, 557 (2023) (Gorsuch, J., concurring).
5. *303 Creative LLC v. Elenis*, 600 U.S. 570, 598 (2023) (Gorsuch, J.).
6. *Coinbase, Inc. v. Bielski*, 599 U.S. 736, 746 (2023) (Kavanaugh, J.).
7. *Dep't of Com. v. New York*, 139 S. Ct. 2551, 2583 (2019) (Breyer, J., concurring in part and dissenting in part).
8. *Jack Daniel's Props, Inc. v. VIP Prods. LLC*, 599 U.S. 140, 145 (2023) (Kagan, J.).
9. *Smith v. Berryhill*, 139 S. Ct. 1765, 1774 (2019) (Sotomayor, J.).

10. *Bank for Sav. v. Collector*, 70 U.S. 495, 504 (1865); Brief for Petitioner, *Alaska Dep't of Env. Cons. v. EPA*, 540 U.S. 461 (2003), 2003 WL 2010655, at *24.

11. *Ruan v. United States*, 597 U.S. 450, 461 (2022) (Breyer, J.).

12. *Pugin v. Garland*, 599 U.S. 600, 624 (2023) (Sotomayor, J., dissenting).

13. *Wilkins v. United States*, 598 U.S. 152, 165 (2023) (Sotomayor, J.).

14. *Kisor v. Wilkie*, 139 S. Ct. 2400, 2413 (2019) (Kagan, J.).

15. *Ysleta Del Sur Pueblo v. Texas*, 596 U.S. 685, 691 (2022) (Gorsuch, J.).

16. *Arizona v. Navajo Nation*, 599 U.S. 555, 565 (2023) (Kavanaugh, J.).

17. *Kisor*, 139 S. Ct. at 2448 (Kavanaugh, J., concurring).

18. *Bittner v. United States*, 598 U.S. 85, 100 (2023) (Gorsuch, J.).

19. *Samia v. United States*, 599 U.S. 635, 657 (2023) (Kagan, J., dissenting).

20. *Biestek v. Berryhill*, 139 S. Ct. 1148, 1154 n.1 (2019) (Kagan, J.).

21. *Bittner*, 598 U.S. at 110 (Barrett, J., dissenting).

22. *Axon Enterprise, Inc. v. FTC*, 598 U.S. 175, 205 (2023) (Gorsuch, J., concurring).

23. *Nat'l Pork Producers Council v. Ross*, 598 U.S. 356, 385 (2023) (Gorsuch, J.).

24. *Dupree v. Younger*, 598 U.S. 729, 737 (2023) (Barrett, J.).

25. *Yegiazaryan v. Smagin*, 599 U.S. 533, 545 (2023) (Sotomayor, J.).

26. *Lac du Flambeau Band of Lake Superior Chippewa Indians v. Coughlin*, 599 U.S. 382, 406 (2023) (Gorsuch, J., dissenting).

27. *NY State Rifle & Pistol Ass'n, Inc. v. Bruen*, 597 U.S. 1, 129 (2022) (Breyer, J., dissenting).

28. *Borden v. United States*, 593 U.S. 420, 432 (2021) (Kagan, J.).

29. *NY State Rifle & Pistol Ass'n, Inc.*, 597 U.S. at 29 (Thomas, J.).

30. *Whole Woman's Health v. Jackson*, 595 U.S. 30, 68 n.3 (2021) (Sotomayor, J., concurring and dissenting).

31. *Andy Warhol Found. for the Visual Arts, Inc.*, 598 U.S. at 530 (Sotomayor, J.).

32. *Fulton v. Philadelphia*, 593 U.S. 522, 543–44 (2021) (Barrett, J., concurring).

33. *Dobbs v. Jackson Women's Health Org.*, 597 U.S. 215, 230 (2022) (Alito, J.).

34. *Students for Fair Admissions, Inc. v. President & Fellows of Harvard Coll.*, 600 U.S. 181, 304 (2023) (Gorsuch, J., concurring).

35. *Id.* at 327 (Sotomayor, J., dissenting).

36. *Wooden v. United States*, 595 U.S. 360, 363–64 (2022) (Kagan, J.).

37. *Haaland v. Brackeen*, 599 U.S. 255, 313 (2023) (Gorsuch, J., concurring).

38. *Navajo Nation*, 599 U.S. at 580 (Gorsuch, J., dissenting).

39. *United States, ex rel. Polansky v. Exec. Health Res., Inc.*, 599 U.S. 419, 427 (2023) (Kagan, J.).

40. *Biden v. Nebraska*, 600 U.S. 477, 525 (2023) (Kagan, J., dissenting).

41. *Id.* at 548.

42. *303 Creative LLC*, 600 U.S. at 629 (Sotomayor, J., dissenting).
43. *Oklahoma v. Castro-Huerta*, 597 U.S. 629, 684 (2022) (Gorsuch, J., dissenting).
44. *Kahler v. Kansas*, 140 S. Ct. 1021, 1031 (2020) (Kagan, J.).
45. *Samia v. United States*, 599 U.S. 635, 659 (2023) (Kagan, J., dissenting).
46. *Andy Warhol Found. for the Visual Arts, Inc.*, 598 U.S. at 581 (Kagan, J., dissenting).

CHAPTER 32

1. *Gundy v. United States*, 139 S. Ct. 2116, 2127 (2019).
2. 12 U.S.C. § 2503(3) (2023).
3. Plainlanguage.gov, Guidelines: Be concise, https://www.plainlanguage.gov/guidelines/concise/keep-the-subject-verb-and-object-close-together/.
4. *Delaware v. Pennsylvania*, 598 U.S. 115, 119 (2023) (Jackson, J.).
5. *Jack Daniel's Props., Inc. v. VIP Prods. LLC*, 599 U.S. 140, 145 (2023) (Kagan, J.).
6. *Jones v. Mississippi*, 593 U.S. 98, 129 (2021) (Sotomayor, J., dissenting).
7. *Sturgeon v. Frost*, 587 U.S. 28, 34 (2019) (Kagan, J.).
8. *Slack Techs., LLC v. Pirani*, 598 U.S. 759, 763 (2023) (Gorsuch, J.).
9. *DHS v. Thuraissigiam*, 140 S. Ct. 1959, 1993 (2020) (Sotomayor, J., dissenting).
10. *Ohio Adjutant Gen.'s Dep't v. FLRA*, 598 U.S. 449, 466 (2023) (Alito, J., dissenting).
11. *Id.* at 468.
12. *Id.* at 469.
13. *Students for Fair Admissions, Inc. v. President & Fellows of Harvard Coll.*, 600 U.S. 181, 393 (2023) (Jackson, J., dissenting).
14. The Court has not used the phrase "mistakes were made" since 1917, referencing a state commission fixing railway rates. *Rowland v. Boyle*, 244 U.S. 106, 110 (1917) (Holmes, J.) ("In fixing the exact rates it may be that mistakes were made.").
15. *Bartenwerfer v. Buckley*, 598 U.S. 69, 72 (2023) (Barrett, J.).
16. *Id.* at 75.
17. *Id.*
18. *Andy Warhol Found. for the Visual Arts, Inc. v. Goldsmith*, 598 U.S. 508, 586 n.10 (2023) (Kagan, J., dissenting).
19. *Id.* at 586.

20. *Fulton v. Philadelphia*, 593 U.S. 522, 614 (2021) (Alito, J., concurring).

21. *Percoco v. United States*, 598 U.S. 319, 330 (2023) (Alito, J.).

22. *Herrera v. Wyoming*, 139 S. Ct. 1686, 1706 (2019) (Alito, J., dissenting).

23. *Bartenwerfer*, 598 U.S. at 75 (Barrett, J.).

24. *Jones*, 593 U.S. at 133 (Sotomayor, J., dissenting).

25. *Mont v. United States*, 139 S. Ct. 1826, 1841 (2019) (Sotomayor, J., dissenting).

26. *Haaland v. Brackeen*, 599 U.S. 255, 350 (2023) (Thomas, J., dissenting).

27. *Id.* at 374 (Alito, J., dissenting).

28. *Glacier Nw., Inc., v. Teamsters*, 598 U.S. 771, 791 (2023) (Jackson, J., dissenting).

29. *Axon Enterprise Inc. v. FTC*, 598 U.S. 175, 211 n.3 (2023) (Gorsuch, J., concurring).

30. *Jack Daniel's Props., Inc.*, 599 U.S. at 144 (Kagan, J.).

31. *Brnovich v. DNC*, 141 S. Ct. 2321, 2354 n.1 (2021) (Kagan, J., dissenting).

32. *Andy Warhol Found. for the Visual Arts, Inc.*, 598 U.S. at 584 (Kagan, J., dissenting).

33. *Jack Daniel's Props., Inc.*, 599 U.S. at 152 (Kagan, J.).

34. *Rucho v. Common Cause*, 139 S. Ct. 2484, 2513 (2019) (Kagan, J., dissenting).

35. *Becerra v. Empire Health Found.*, 597 U.S. 424, 430 (2022) (Kagan, J.).

36. *West Virginia v. EPA*, 597 U.S. 697, 779 (2022) (Kagan, J., dissenting).

37. *Torres v. Madrid*, 592 U.S. 306, 315 (2021) (Roberts, C. J.).

38. *Id.* at 310.

39. *Taniguchi v. Kan Pac. Saipan, Ltd.*, 566 U.S. 560, 566 (2012) (Alito, J.); *Id.* at 576 (Ginsburg, J., dissenting).

40. *Flowers v. Mississippi*, 139 S. Ct. 2228, 2253 (2019) (Thomas, J., dissenting).

41. *Edwards v. Vannoy*, 593 U.S. 255, 302 (2021) (Kagan, J., dissenting).

42. *Dubin v. United States*, 599 U.S. 110, 133 (2023) (Gorsuch, J., concurring).

43. *Florida v. Georgia*, 592 U.S. 433, 439 (2021) (Barrett, J.)

44. *Andy Warhol Found. for the Visual Arts, Inc.*, 598 U.S. at 576 (Kagan, J., dissenting).

45. *Lange v. California*, 141 S. Ct. 2011, 2028 (2021) (Roberts, C.J., concurring).

46. *Becerra*, 597 U.S. at 439 (Kagan, J.).

47. *Jack Daniel's Props., Inc.*, 599 U.S. at 157 (Kagan, J.).

48. *Health & Hosp. Corp. of Marion Cnty. v. Talevski*, 599 U.S. 166, 172 (2023) (Jackson, J.).

49. *Biden v. Texas*, 597 U.S. 785, 806 (2022) (Roberts, C. J.).

50. *Percoco v. United States*, 598 U.S. 319, 336 (2023) (Gorsuch, J., concurring).

51. *Calcutt v. FDIC*, 598 U.S. 623, 624 (2023) (per curiam).

CLOSING

1. President Barack Obama, *State of the Union Address* (Jan. 20, 2015), https://obamawhitehouse.archives.gov/the-press-office/2015/01/20/remarks-president-state-union-address-January-20-2015.

2. Rensselaer Polytech. Inst., *A Conversation with Chief Justice John G. Roberts, Jr.*, YouTube, at 20:20 (April 12, 2017), https://www.youtube.com/watch?v=TuZEKlRgDEg.

3. *Id.*

4. *Id.*

5. *Brown v. Bd. of Ed.*, 347 U.S. 483, 495 (1954) (Warren, J.).

Index

For the benefit of digital users, indexed terms that span two pages (e.g., 52–53) may, on occasion, appear on only one of those pages.